Grund- und Leistungskurs Englisch

Friedhold Schmidt
T. Lothar Wullen

Young People in an Adult World

Max Hueber Verlag

1. Auflage

3. 2. 1. | Die letzten Ziffern
1985 84 83 82 81 | bezeichnen Zahl und Jahr des Druckes.
Alle Drucke dieser Auflage können nebeneinander benutzt werden.

Typographische Gestaltung: U. Langbein, München
Umschlaggestaltung: Jock und Elspeth Kinneir
Gesamtherstellung: Manz AG, Dillingen · Printed in Germany
ISBN 3–19–00.2285–2

Inhaltsverzeichnis

Vorwort

Bei der Erstellung der vorliegenden Sammlung haben sich die Herausgeber zum Ziel gesetzt, einen Einblick in die vielschichtige Problematik der Adoleszenz als Übergangszeit zwischen Kindheit und Erwachsenenalter zu vermitteln. Da sich die primäre Zielgruppe, die Schüler der Sekundarstufe II (Kollegstufe), in dieser Phase des Umbruchs befindet, dürfte die Thematik im Grund- und Leistungskurs auf besonderes Interesse stoßen und zu vielfältigen Diskussionen Anlaß bieten.

Die Sammlung ist gleichermaßen für den Grundkurs und den Leistungskurs geeignet, da – entsprechend den curricularen Zielvorstellungen – Texte verschiedenen Schwierigkeitsgrades ausgewählt und die Aufgabenstellungen nicht entsprechend den beiden Kursarten differenziert wurden. Für den Grundkurs müßte wegen der geringeren Stundenzahl nach den Vorstellungen des Fachlehrers, bzw. dem Leistungsstand der Lerngruppe, eine Auswahl aus der vorliegenden Sammlung getroffen werden. In jedem Fall jedoch sollte die Behandlung des Themas durch mindestens eine literarische Ganzschrift ergänzt werden. Dazu eignen sich u. a. folgende Autoren/Werke:

Roman: St. Barstow, *A Kind of Loving;* B. Bainbridge, *Harriet Said;* G. Cain, *Blueschild Baby;* Ch. Dickens, *Great Expectations;* H. Fielding, *Joseph Andrews;* W. Golding, *Lord of the Flies; The Pyramid;* B. Hines, *Kes;* E. Hunter, *Blackboard Jungle;* J. Joyce, *A Portrait of the Artist;* J. Kerouac, *On the Road;* D. H. Lawrence, *Sons and Lovers;* H. Lee, *To Kill a Mockingbird;* L. Lee, *Cider with Rosie; As I Walked Out One Midsummer Morning;* P. Roth, *Good-bye Columbus;* J. Salinger, *Catcher in the Rye;* A. Sillitoe, *The Loneliness of the Long-distance Runner;* D. Storey, *This Sporting Life;* V. Woolf, *To the Lighthouse;* J. Wain, *The Contenders;* Ch. Webb, *The Graduate.*

Short Story: St. Barstow, *The Desperadoes and other stories;* S. Hill, *A Bit of Singing and Dancing;* J. C. Oates, *Where are you going? Where have you been?* F. O'Connor, *Masculine Protest and other stories; Day Dreams and other stories;* J. Salinger, *Nine Stories; Franny and Zooey;* A. Sillitoe, *The Ragman's Daughter.*

Drama: E. Bond, *Saved;* S. Delaney, *A Taste of Honey;* B. Friel, *Philadelphia, Here I Come!* B. Keefe, *Gimme Shelter;* E. O'Neill, *Ah, Wilderness;* J. Osborne, *Look Back in Anger;* T. Rattigan, *The Winslow Boy;* P. Shaffer, *Five Finger Exercise; Equus;* W. Shakespeare, *As You Like It; Romeo and Juliet;* B. Shaw, *Major Barbara;* J. M. Synge, *The Playboy of the Western World;* A. Wesker, *Chips with Everything;* T. Williams, *The Glass Menagerie.*

Die Auswahl der Texte erfolgte unter Berücksichtigung dreier Kriterien. Einmal wurde eine ausgewogene Mischung fiktionaler und nicht fiktionaler Texte angestrebt. Zum andern wurde streng auf eine breite Fächerung der verschiedenen Textsorten *(poetry, short story, novel, drama, essay, report, cartoon, advertisement, letter)* geachtet. Ferner waren die Herausgeber bemüht, möglichst nur solche literarischen Texte einzubeziehen, die bisher dem Englischunterricht nicht oder nur selten zugänglich gemacht wurden.

Alle Texte wurden mit einem Aufgabenapparat versehen, der den in den einzelnen Bundesländern vorherrschenden Zielvorstellungen für die Reifeprüfung und deren Vorbereitung möglichst weitgehend entspricht. Dieser Apparat ist zunächst in *Text analysis* und *Exercises* unterteilt. Unter *Text analysis* werden Informationsaufnahme, -verarbeitung und -bewertung sowie problemlösendes Denken anhand von *Comprehension, Structure and Style* und *Appreciation and Comment* eingeübt. Hierbei wurde insbesondere auch auf die Integration der Linguistik zur Beschreibung der Sprache und des Stils Wert gelegt; gleichzeitig wurde durch die Art der Aufgabenstellungen eine Progression innerhalb der Sammlung angestrebt. Die *Exercises* dienen der mündlichen wie schriftlichen Textproduktion im Rahmen von *summary-writing, essay, interpretation, letter-writing, discussion, role-play, creative writing.*

Herausgeber und Verlag

I.
Definition

1. The Nature of Adolescence

An adolescent is the product of the interaction of his biological heritage and the culture in which he lives. The adolescent is a product of his culture because he has spent the years of his childhood as a participant in that culture; has, figuratively speaking, sat as a child upon the knee of his culture. It is now a common assumption of cultural anthropologists, psychologists, sociologists, and others who deal with the problems of human behavior that the years of an individual's childhood are of exceeding importance in creating the kind of person he is. The only controversy involved, insofar as differences of opinion exist, is in how large terms one interprets the term "exceeding." In any event the individual may not be considered apart from the structure of the society in which he lives including every perceived element in it.

Adolescence, as it is generally used, is a descriptive term of the period during which an emotionally immature individual in his teens approaches the culmination of his physical and mental growth. Although potentially an adult, he still plays the role of an inexperienced child bound and restricted by the culture in which he lives. In its nonphysical aspects adolescence is culturally determined and represents a period of difficult adjustment if the environment is a restrictive one. In a nonrestrictive environment the adolescent's problems tend to be primarily those of gaining and applying experience.

In a culture, as in some existing primitive ones, in which early responsibility and status are accorded to youth, the period of adolescence may be attenuated or greatly simplified. In contrast, the period of adolescence in Western culture is more complex and more beset by problems. This complexity is due in part to lack of emancipation from parents, vocational dependence and extension of training, sex restrictions and taboos, and inferior status. However, it is recognized that the ease or difficulty of the transition from childhood through adolescence into adulthood is a function of the amount of facilitation the culture offers to the individual who is going through the transitional period. The greater the facilitation, the easier the transition.

In former years adolescence was alleged to be inevitably a period of great and excessive storm and stress; it was supposed to represent a complete and sudden "rebirth" and change of personality. According to this point of view, difficulty during adolescence was held to be inevitable. The theory of storm and stress has been abandoned today. It is now believed that adolescence is culturally determined, that the amount of difficulty is a direct function of the restrictiveness of the environment, and to only a very small degree a function of biological change within the individual.

A true understanding of adolescence includes a recognition of the existence of individual differences. Surface similarities may often conceal crucial differences. It must be remembered that even if two or more adolescents are in similar physical environments, their psychological environments are not necessarily also similar. It is a mistake to generalize too broadly about adolescence from experience with it in any given environment, even within a fairly homogeneous culture. Intracultural differences do exist, such as differences caused by technological change, climate, historical period, socio-economic status, and literally thousands of other factors. Not only do adolescents differ with different environments, but an adolescent who moves from one environment to another will also display certain differences from his former self. The depression and the period of World War II are examples of historical changes that reflected upon the problems and ways of life of those who were adolescents during the 1930's and early 1940's.

An understanding of a given adolescent requires a wide and extensive knowledge of his past as well as his present physical and psychological environments. He must be viewed as an adolescent, but he must also be viewed as a human being, and his behavior as an adolescent must be interpreted with the aid of that view.

In Western culture there are five points of reference from which to view adolescent growth and development:

1. It is a time of physical development and growth.
2. It is a time when group relations become of major importance.
3. Adolescence is a time of seeking status as an individual.
4. It is a time of intellectual expansion, development, and academic experience.
5. It is a time of development and evaluation of values.

Adolescence is viewed as a period of adjustment to cultural demands; and of expectations as to commonalities of behavior and development, within which individual differences may also be expected.

Vocabulary

biological heritage (= Erbanlagen) – *controversy* [kən'trɔvəsi] prolonged argument, difference of opinion – *to perceive* to notice – *to accord* (fml) to grant, to give – *to attenuate* (fml) to weaken, to reduce – *beset by* troubled by – *facilitation* from: *to facilitate* to make easier – *to allege* to claim

Text analysis

Comprehension

1. To what extent do scientists agree/disagree about the influence of culture on the adolescent?
2. What is the author's definition of adolescence?
3. In what way does adolescence vary from culture to culture?
4. What is the theory of storm and stress and what is its relevance today?
5. Why is it a mistake to generalize too broadly about adolescents even within one culture?

Structure and style

6. Describe the logical development of the author's ideas.
7. Characterize the last section of the text and describe its function.
8. Try to describe the author's choice of words (lexis). Draw up a list of words closely related to the subject matter.
   On the basis of your list explain why the lexis must be called formal rather than informal, and special (technical) rather than non-special (non-technical).

Text form

9. The above text is a piece of scientific writing, which characteristically makes use of formal and technical lexis. It also makes use of a particular kind of sentence structure (syntax). Try to describe the syntax by means of the following statements:

	True	False
a) The sentences are rather complex[1] on the whole		
b) The sentences are rather simple on the whole		
c) The sentences are grammatically complete		
d) Many sentences are grammatically incomplete (elliptical)		
e) The text contains many weak forms (isn't, don't etc)		
f) The text contains no weak forms		
h) The sentences are relatively short		
i) The sentences are relatively long		

Appreciation and comment

10. Do you share the author's opinion that the adolescent is an "emotionally immature individual"? Give reasons.
11. Which of the five points of reference mentioned do you consider as most important and why?

Exercises

1. Write a summary of the text by reducing each paragraph to two sentences only.
2. Write a passage explaining in some detail what you understand by "lack of emancipation from parents, vocational dependence and extension of training, sex restriction and taboos, and inferior status".

---

[1]) Make sure you are familiar with the grammatical terms *simple, complex, compound* with reference to sentences. Cf. e.g. R. A. Close, *A Reference Grammar for Students of English,* London, 1975; D. Crystal / D. Davy, *Investigating English Style,* London, 1969.

Age limits 2

age you have a right to

5

Go to school

7

Withdraw money from a post office savings account

10

Be convicted of a criminal offence provided prosecution can prove you knew what you were doing

13

Buy fireworks
Be employed for certain hours a week
Buy a pet animal
Be fingerprinted if in custody charged with an offence

14

Be convicted if you are male of a sexual or unnatural offence (also before this age in certain circumstances)
Own an air rifle
Take part in a public performance without a licence
Be held fully responsible for a crime
Pawn an article at a pawn shop
Play cribbage or dominoes in a room in a pub which is not a bar

15

Possess an assembled shot-gun if under the supervision of someone over twenty-one

16

Invest in Premium Bonds
Sell scrap metal
Join a trade union
Leave school
Choose your own doctor
Apply for social security benefit
Work full time
Age of consent for sexual intercourse (girls)
Leave home, with parents' consent

16

Enter, or live in, a brothel
Marry, with parents' consent
Hold a licence to drive certain tractors, ride a motorcyle and invalid carriage
Enter the bar of a pub but not buy a drink unless you are also buying a meal in which case you can order beer and wine

17

Hold a licence to drive any vehicle except certain heavy vehicles
Enter a betting shop
Buy or hire firearms and hold a licence to possess a firearm
Apply for a private pilot's licence
Engage in street trading

18

Age of majority
Leave home
Marry
Vote
Bring and defend accusations in court
Act as executor or administrator of a deceased person's estate
Make a will
Change your name
Apply for a passport on your own responsibility
Buy and sell goods
Enter into hire purchase agreements
Apply for a mortgage
Be a full legal owner of house and land
Sue and be sued in the courts
Go abroad for the purpose of singing, playing, performing or being part of an exhibition without a licence
Buy drinks in the bar of a pub

18

Pay adult contributions to National Insurance schemes
Sit on a jury
Do almost anything an adult can do except

21

Be a candidate in a parliamentary or local election
Hold a licence to drive any mechanically propelled vehicle
Hold a licence to sell intoxicating liquor

Vocabulary

prosecution (= Staatsanwaltschaft) – *custody* arrest for investigation – *to pawn* to deposit valuables as guarantee for money borrowed – *cribbage* card game – *Premium Bonds* (= Prämiensparpapier) – *brothel* (= Bordell) – *deceased* [di'si:st] dead – *mortgage* ['mɔgidʒ] (= Hypothek) – *to sue* to take to court

Text analysis

1. How are the age limits presented?
2. Comment on the language used.
3. Discuss to what extent the restrictions seem appropriate to you.
4. Point out some of the differences in the legal position of young people in England and in your country.

3 *Adolescents and Adults*

Adolescents have a strong tendency to resist authority and, therefore, often want to do the opposite of what they are asked. This is tied up with their desire to be recognized as individuals and their breaking loose from shackles. They want to choose their own friends, amusements, clothes and books. The parents' reluctance to grant this independence and their efforts to pry into the affairs of their children, their refusal to allow them a key, so that they know when they come in (and can ask where they have been), their failure to trust – all lead to constant friction.

Another important reason for friction is the fact that the adolescent is beginning to think for himself. Whereas previously he had accepted what his parents said, he now wants to have good reasons for their edicts. He questions their infallibility, and they do not like it. They are not accustomed to having their word questioned. One frequent reply, 'Because I say so', does not go down well with the intelligent adolescent. Parents dislike having their authority questioned. When a child on being reprimanded begins to try to explain his actions, his father snaps, 'Don't argue! Don't answer back!'

Other features of the adolescent which lead to friction at home are his tendency to withdraw from the family circle into seclusion, his scathing comments and sarcasm directed at his brothers and sisters, his selfishness, the girl's choice of clothes, hair-styles and boyfriends, and the boy's accusations, when thwarted in his desires, that his parents are 'horrible'.

Adults, too, have their personality problems. Much of the friction with children is due to their parents' intolerance, impatience and bad temper. Some teachers become angry with a child who is slow to learn. Parents are impatient when the child fails to understand instructions given to him, or forgets what he has been told to do. They shout at a child who breaks a plate forgetting that he is more clumsy in his movements than an adult.

Another cause of friction is failure to appreciate the sensitiveness of the adolescent. He is readily offended by comments about his appearance and dirty face, and infuriated at parents' criticism of his friends. He particularly resents being reprimanded in front of his brothers or sisters. He hates to feel that derogatory remarks are being made about him as soon as his back is turned.

On the other hand, parents feel thwarted because of their failure to stop various habits and forms of behaviour in their adolescent children. They lose their temper when their son cannot be made to be tidy; when he will not stop blinking his eyes, shrugging his shoulders, stuttering; when he looks stupid in front of strangers, because of his shyness; when he is ridiculously jealous for no good reason; when he refuses to admit to a theft or breakage. It infuriates the parents because they totally fail to stop their children doing these things.

Vocabulary

shackle band for fastening around the wrist or ankle (of an animal or person) – *reluctance* unwillingness – *to pry into* to inquire with too much interest – *edict* ['iːdikt] order – *infallibility* quality of never making mistakes – *to reprimand* to blame for s.th. – *to snap* to say quickly (and angrily) – *seclusion* state of being separate from other people – *scathing* bitterly cruel – *to thwart* to oppose, to frustrate – *derogatory* showing lack of respect – *to blink* to shut and open the eye quickly

Text analysis

Comprehension

1. Why according to the author do young people often resist authority?
2. How do parents usually react to their children questioning their infallibility?
3. What is the adolescent's relation to his family?
4. What criticism about adults does the author voice?
5. Why are parents often frustrated?

Structure and style

6. Analyse the logical build-up of the text.
7. Make a list of the words and expressions that help to structure the text.
8. What use does the author make of words that belong to formal style? Make a list of them.
9. To what extent are complex sentences to be found in the text?

Text form

10. Study question 9 of text No. 1 and explain whether the above text is also to be considered as scientific writing. Give reasons.

Appreciation and comment

11. To what extent do you share the author's view about the conflicts between adolescents and adults?
12. Parents and children should be more considerate of each other. Discuss.

Exercises

1. Write a summary of the text not exceeding 150 words.
2. Make a list of "dos" and "don'ts" for parents and adolescents. E.g. "Adults should/should not . . ."

4 They don't speak our language

This essay is intended to transmit the message that teenage groups are still basically expressing class values. Dress, hair-style, heroes, and haunts may change along with the labels, but the basic values remain similar. The argot is often concerned with descriptions of dress and with particular experiences of that teenage group. However, drugs and adult ideologies have altered some of the traditional class values and this is reflected in the degree of variation of the argot from the vernacular.

What I have attempted to show is that teenagers have a life outside of school which has its own rules, language and system of values, and that these are enmeshed together. Inevitably such a network of interrelating and interlocking factors spills over into school in the sense that the teenagers who still have to come to school do not, cannot, leave their affiliations (social class, age, group or gang, values etc.) at the school gate to be picked up again at the end of school. Often schools try to make teenagers leave their affiliations at home by the expedient of not allowing teenage 'gear' into schools. But whether the teenage gear is banned or not–and anyway it is only the outward and visible signs of an inward and invisible commitment–teenagers have outside affiliations which they bring into school. In fact the battle that goes on in some schools over teenage gear perhaps highlights the entrenched attitudes that can exist on both sides. Teachers and teenagers see teenage 'culture' as something to be fought over. Teenage gear is one such *casus belli.* Another is the language of teenagers.

Concerning the language of teenagers, teachers see such language as antipathetic: teenage language is 'slovenly' and is full of terms which the adult cannot and is not supposed to understand. It embodies a system of values which teachers may feel threatens their own; it is used against teachers deliberately to exclude them. This could be said to be a view of a teacher dealing daily with teenagers at school. But an examination of the view from the teenagers' point will be of value here. Teenagers feel threatened by the constant pressure exerted on them by adults to conform to adult values, adult language and adult affiliations. Teachers have to realize (and many have) that experiences provided by the school are not the only ones in the life of a teenager. Teachers might also realize that the expression of values in behaviour is not exclusively to do with being a teenager, but also with social class differences.

What I have written about is in a sense historical, but I hope that what I have had to say about teenage groups gives some insights into the meaning of teenage behaviour which have continuity. By concentrating on the language of teenage groups it is possible to see that what the special languages of the groups embody are different sets or systems of values. When these values change, and they are harder to change than organizational structures, then it will be possible to see the new meanings expressed in the new language which will be needed. Thus the continuing interest and usefulness of considering the language of teenage groups.

Vocabulary

haunt place frequented – *argot* ['a:gəu] special language of a group – *vernacular* dialect – *enmeshed* (here:) closely linked – *affiliation* [əfili'eiʃən] connection – *expedient* means – *gear* (sl.) clothes – *commitment* (= Bindung, Verpflichtung) – *entrenched* deep-rooted – *slovenly* careless, slipshod – *insight into* understanding of

Text analysis

Comprehension

1. What is the relation between the language of teenagers, class, and the vernacular?
2. According to the author, what friction is there between teenagers and school? What is its cause?
3. What are the characteristics of teenage language and what attitude should teachers adopt towards it?
4. What is the purpose of this essay?

Structure and style

5. Reduce the text to notes that mirror its logical structure. Do not use complete sentences.
6. What lexical features mark the text as a socio-linguistic study?
7. What markers of formal style does the text contain?

Text form

8. The above text is a socio-linguistic study. Determine whether it is complete in itself or not. If you consider it to be an extract, try to establish its position within the larger context.

Appreciation and comment

9. The author assumes that class distinctions are reflected in the behaviour and language of teenagers. Do you share his view as far as your own country is concerned? Give reasons.
10. To what extent should schools try to influence teenage group behaviour?
11. In what way should schools make allowances for the social background of their pupils?

Exercises

1. Write a brief summary of the above text.
2. Should schools be permitted to regulate their students' outward appearance in class? Discuss.

II.
Identification

Growing up

5

One morning, when I was fifteen, I got up before daybreak, because all night I hadn't been able to sleep, left my bed quietly in the darkness of early morning and put on my clothes, a blue cotton shirt, a pair of corduroy pants, stocking and shoes. It was November and it was beginning to turn cold, but I did not wish to put on more clothes. I felt warm enough. I felt almost feverish, and with more clothes I knew it would not happen. Something was going to happen, and I felt that if I put on too much clothes it would dwindle away and all that I would have would be the remembrance of something expected, then lost.

I walked quietly through the darkness of the house and emerged, standing for a moment in the street, acknowledging the magnificence of our earth. Merely to be standing, merely to be breathing that day was a truth in the nature of an inexplicable miracle. After all these years, I thought . . . I myself standing here in the darkness, breathing, knowing that I live. I wanted to say something in language, with the words I had been taught in school, something solemn and dignified and joyous . . . to express the gratitude I felt to God. But it was impossible. There were no words with which to say it. I could feel the magnificence coming through the cold clean air, touching my blood, racing through it, dancing, but there were no words with which to say it.

There was a fire hydrant in our street, and I had always wanted to hurdle it, but I had always been afraid to try. The hydrant, leaping swiftly, my flesh would smash against it, paining me, perhaps breaking a bone in one of my legs.

Suddenly I was leaping over the hydrant, and, clearing it, I was thinking, I can do it now, I can do anything now.

I hurdled the fire hydrant six or seven times, leaping away over it, hearing myself landing solidly on the earth, feeling tremendous.

Then I began to walk, not slowly, not casually, but vigorously, leaping now and then because I couldn't help it. Each time I came to a tree, I leaped and caught a limb, making it bend with my weight, pulling myself up and letting myself down. I walked into the town, into the streets where we had put up our buildings, and suddenly I saw them for this first time, suddenly I was really *seeing* them, and they were splendid. The city was almost deserted, and I alone in it, its only inhabitant, seeing it as it really was, in all its fineness, with all its meaning, giving it its real truth. The winter sun came up while I walked and its light fell over the city, making a cool warmth. I touched the buildings, feeling them with the palms of my hands, feeling the meaning of the solidity and the precision. I touched the plate-glass windows, the brick, the wood and the cement.

When I got home, everyone was awake, at the breakfast table. Where have you been? they asked. Why did you get up so early?

I sat in my chair at the table, feeling great hunger. Shall I tell them? I thought. Shall I try to tell them what is happening? Will they understand? Or will they laugh at me?

Suddenly I knew I was a stranger among them, my own people, and I knew that while I loved them, I could not go out to them, revealing the truth of my being. Each of us is alone, I thought. Each is a stranger to the other. My mother thinks of me as a pain she once suffered, a babe at her breast, a small child in the house, a boy walking to school, and now a young man with an ugly face, a restless and half-mad fellow who moves about strangely.

No, I thought. I cannot tell them. I cannot tell anyone. Everyone must see for himself. Everyone must seek the truth for himself. It is here, and each man must seek it for himself.

I went for a little walk, I replied.

Everyone began to laugh at me, even my mother. What's the matter with you? they asked. Why can't you sleep? Are you in love again? Is that it? Are you dreaming of some girl?

I sat at the table, swallowing the hot food, hearing their laughter. I cannot tell them, I thought. They are laughing at me. They think it is something to laugh about. They think it is a little joke.

I began to blush. Yes, they laughed. It must be some girl. Look how handsome he is getting to be. Dreaming about a girl always does that.

I got up from the table. If I try to tell the truth, I thought, they will laugh more than ever.

I'm going to school, I said, and I left the house. But I knew I would not go to school that day. I had decided not to go in the middle of the night, when I had been unable to sleep. In school, in that atmosphere, it would never happen. I would never be able to understand what it was that turned in me, circling toward truth, and it would be lost, maybe forever. I decided to walk into the country and be alone with the thought, helping it to emerge from the bewilderment and confusion of my mind, and the fever of my blood, carrying it to silence and simplicity, giving it a chance to reach its fullness and be whole.

Walking through the country, moving quietly among the leafless grape vines and fig trees, the thought became whole, and I knew the truth about myself and man and the earth and God.

At the proper hour I returned home, as if I were coming home from school, and the following day I went to school. After the roll was taken, my name was called and our teacher said: You were not at school yesterday. Have you brought an excuse?

No, I said, I have not.

Suddenly I felt myself to be the object of the laughter of everyone in the classroom, and I could imagine everyone thinking: What a stupid fellow! I hadn't intended to entertain anyone, and the laughter made me angry.

Why were you away from school? said the teacher. Where were you?

I was in the country, I said, walking.

Now the laughter was greater than ever, and I saw the girl I secretly loved laughing with the others, as if I meant nothing to her. I began to feel ill and defiant, and there was warm perspiration on the palms of my hands. And I knew I would never be able to speak to the girl about my love for her, and the meaning of that love to me, and to the earth and the universe, and to man.

I was sent to the principal of the school, and he stood over me, grumbling in a deep voice. You, he said, you are a disgrace to this school. You break rules. Then you come to school flaunting your crime. What have you to say for yourself?

Nothing, I said.

Why did you do it? he asked.

I wanted to walk, I said.

You could have waited till Saturday, he said.

No, I said. I had to walk yesterday.

Can you think of any reason why I shouldn't strap you? he asked.

That's up to you, I said.

The strapping made me cry, big as I was, strong as I was. While I cried, though, I knew it wasn't the strapping that was hurting me . . . it was this other thing, this incredible blindness everywhere. I cried bitterly, and when I returned to class my eyes were red and I was ashamed, and the whole class was laughing at me, even the girl.

After school, walking alone, I tried to heal the wound in my heart, and I began to think again of the swift and bright truth of being, the truth I had earned for myself by walking alone through the silence of the earth, and walking, thinking of it, I could feel myself becoming whole again, and I could hear myself laughing through the vastness of the secret space I had discovered.

I had seen the universe, quietly in the emptiness, secret, and I had revealed it to itself, giving it meaning and grace and the truth that could come only from the thought and energy of man, and the truth was man, myself, moment after moment, and man, century after century, and man, and the face of God in man, and the sound of the laughter of man in the vastness of the secret, and the sound of his weeping in the darkness of it, and the truth was myself and I was man.

Vocabulary

corduroy ['kɔːdərɔi] (= Cord) – *to dwindle* to become gradually smaller – *to emerge* to come out, to come into view – *inexplicable* [iniks'plikəbl] not to be explained – *miracle* ['mirəkl] wonder – *to hurdle s.th.* to jump over – *to leap* to jump – *limb* branch of a tree – *plate-glass* fine clear glass in thick sheets for use in windows – *grape-vine* (= Rebstock) – *fig* (= Feige) – *roll* (here:) list of students – *defiant* trotzig – *perspiration* sweat – *palm* inner part of o.'s hand – *principal* head of a school or college – *to flaunt* to show for admiration s.th. one is proud of – *to strap* to beat

Text analysis

Comprehension

1. Why was the boy so excited one November morning and what did his excitement lead to?
2. What were his feelings after he had left the house?
3. Why was the fire hydrant so important to him?
4. What impression did the town make on him?
5. Describe what happened at the breakfast table after he had come home.
6. Why did he play truant and how did the others react?
7. In what way did the incidents influence him?

Structure and style

8. To what extent is the story structured by description, narration, and dialogue?
9. What is the point of view employed in the story and how does it affect its meaning?
10. What do lexis and syntax contribute towards the presentation of character?
11. Outline the significance of the setting.

Text form

12. A short story often presents a decisive experience in a person's life. Discuss to what extent this is also true of the above story.

Appreciation and comment

13. Examine and explain the significance of symbolism in the story.
14. Describe the attitudes of the grown-ups towards the boy's behaviour. Do you share their views?

15. Whereas young people often claim that adults do not understand them, adults, in turn, say that young people need guidance. Discuss.

Exercises

1. Make a list of words from the story that express feeling. Categorise them according to word classes.
2. Write a short passage on a situation in which you felt that adults did not understand you.

6

Mods

Most Mods will tell you that Mods never disappeared; but they did; or at least they dropped out of the popular imagination. The 1960s Mods were bred into a different and more optimistic world. Their clothes were inspired by America's West Coast and the West Indies; their music came from the Rude Boys of Jamaica, Ska, Blue Beat and, into the United States, from the black music of Detroit, Atlanta and Chicago. It grew into something uniquely English and, in the early stages, was a London phenomenon, stretching out tentacles to the coastal resorts at weekends and bank holidays, to the disapproval of the media.

Different Mods took different routes. 'You know how it took off for me?' recalled a retired 1960s Mod. 'The cover of the second Rolling Stones EP, with Jagger in a striped jumper . . .' Today, viewing the Stones as inspiration borders on blasphemy: they belong to a world of money, superstardom and Rock, which isn't Mod.

Then there's The Who, with their name emblazoned across a thousand newly-purchased Army surplus Parka coats. But for the serious Mod they are at best old men, a memory. At 28, Barry, number one in the Crewe Jaguars scooter club and a veteran of 12 years, is caustic. 'Without us The Who would have been nothing. I listened to them then, but they've gone now. They're into rock music, not our kind of music at all . . .'

Mods were dying out in London by the late 1960s. Swamped by hippies and locked in an expensive clothes race they collapsed, almost under the weight of mohair. For modern Mod chroniclers, like 21-year-olds Kim Gault and Clive Reems, who manage the band Back to Zero and produce a Mod fanzine *Maximum Speed*, the subsequent history was simple. 'There were three kinds of Mod, the scooter lot in Parkas, the trendy Mods and the hard Mods. The hard Mods turned into Skinheads,' said Kim Gault.

In the south, the Skins have survived, ever since, with their own rigidly defined fashions: Levi Staprest trousers, braces, boots.

The last Resort is a clothes shop. It resembles a King's Road punk shop, but it's in Goulston Street, in Spitalfields, and its clientele are young working-class Punks, Mods and Skins, co-existing in relative harmony. No Teds or greasers come near. Parkas hang on a rack outside. Inside the shop is neon and blue paint. Inflatable torsos and legs dangle from the ceiling. A statue of Marilyn Monroe, her dress frozen in the classic still from 'Seven Year Itch', dominates one corner.

Eddie Guy, a 21-year-old labourer from Poplar, told me: 'I've been a Mod for a couple of months. I like the fashion. I used to be a Punk but I gave it up because of the rows I had with my parents.' These days things like that matter. And as another Mod said: 'Would you offer someone a job if they've got pins through their noses, and ears, and cheeks?' Indeed, one of the great Mod obsessions is still neatness. 'We're different to the average person, but to an extent we conform,' a member of the 5–15s, a scooter club, told me at Sevenoaks. 'You can't beat a smart person, can you?'

When Punk blasted a hole through the big-business-controlled youth culture in the mid-1970s, not everyone wanted to march through the breach. The Killermeters, a Mod band from Huddersfield formed last winter, had experimented with Punk, but became fed up with it. They work some gigs in London now, and suggest that up north Punk maybe getting bigger. As Vic Vespa, their lead singer, explained: 'They're always a few years behind times when it comes to music.'

Indeed, this 'backwardness' partly explains why Mods north of Birmingham have their own separate history. Far from the London of the late 1960s, the Mod scene survived, albeit in a heretical form. Expensive clothes were less important, and alcohol rivalled amphetamines. The search for a different identity led to increasingly obscure American soul records and dancing, especially dancing. In the early 1970s, Northern Soul was born, which centred on allnight dances in Cleethorpes, Manchester, and above all, Wigan.

But Northern Soul was corrupted. Radio One noticed it, audiences became younger, cops were overenthusiastic, journalists wrote articles about it. Yet this regional youth culture survived, with its own records, clothes, and, far more than the effete South, its own scooters. Fragments of the old Mod culture were preserved, and there is now fierce resistance against Southerners threatening to take it away again.

The new Mods of London are unaware of the rancour. Sitting in the Dublin Castle pub in Camden Town, Marcelle, an 18-year-old nurse, sipped her Pernod and lemonade and explained her escape from Disco and her conversion to the Mods. 'Here, you are part of the scene, part of the elite. Of course up North there are loads of Mods,' she added blithely, 'but scooters are the only thing they are into.'

The northern Mods made their own demonstration of this one weekend in July when they arrived in the North Wales resort of Rhyl. It was the destination of a run. Runs are, and always have been, part of the Mod mythology. Pass the word, get on your scooter and head for the coast with your 'club'. There are the Scunthorpe Road Rats, the Crewe Jaguars, the Preston Wild Cats, the Burnley and Pendle Scooter Club . . . even a tiny delegation from the South's 5–15s. The weekend achieved some Press coverage, and was labelled a riot. It wasn't.

In the Palace Hotel, Rhyl, at opening time, Brad, a 20-year-old Yorkshire Mod, explains what makes him and his friends different from the new Southern Mods. 'When we were coming back from Brighton,' he says, 'we stopped at Bishop's Stortford. There were all these Mods wearing Parkas with 'The Who' on them, but they had no Lambrettas or Vespas. 'They were just posers. Mind you,' he added, 'there's no hassle between us and the 5–15s. If you ride a scooter and go on runs you're OK as far as we're concerned. Scooter is first, then clothes and music.'

The scooter clubs, of course, after years of recession are on the rise again. They are open to anyone over 17 (the legal minimum age for a scooter licence), who is accepted by the committee, and shows up for runs. They even have loan schemes for Mods on hard times.

Rhyl's Mod Saturday is moving into the night. In the bay window of a pub sits Ritchie Andrews, a local, and veteran of the 1960s. Unlike Barry he has long since abandoned his scooter; he drives a Ford Lotus Cortina Mk 1 and is unrepentant.

What does he feel about all the youthful disciples crowding the bar? 'Mod was a *culture*. This is a sham of what happened years ago.' He waved at the multitude. 'Look round this room. Now they are wearing what I can only describe as cheap clothes. Then, if you went out in a new suit you wouldn't sit down all night! You know why? Because you'd crease it. I've got a lot of respect for the clubs, but the scooter fanatic of 18 to 20 really doesn't know what it's all about. They don't. It isn't *impossible* to be a Mod, they just go about it in the wrong way. A scooter was a means of transport, you didn't hero-worship it.'

Vocabulary

phenomenon [fi'nɔminən] – *tentacle* ['tentəkl] feeler of an animal for testing and catching – *to border on blasphemy* ['blæsfimi] to be almost an insult – *to emblazon* to put decoratively on – *surplus* ['sə:pləs] additional to what is needed – *caustic* bitter, sharp – *to swamp* to flood – *chronicler* person keeping a record of s.th. – *fanzine* fan magazine – *inflatable* capable of beeing filled with air – *still* photograph advertising movie film – *breach* opening – *gig* (sl.) engagement to play music – *amphetamine* [æm'fitəmin] – *effete* [e'fi:t] weak, worn out – *rancour* bitterness, hatred – *elite* [ei'li:t] – *blithe* happy, joyous – *hassle* quarrel – *on hard times* in financial difficulties – *unrepentant* not sorry for wrongdoing – *sham* not real, not genuine

Text analysis

Comprehension

1. What was characteristic of the mods in the 1960s?
2. What happened to the mods in the late 1960s and to what extent have they survived?
3. What relation is there between Mods and Punks?
4. Why was the development in the north different from that in the rest of the country?
5. What is Ritchie Andrews' opinion of the new mods?

Structure and style

6. Subdivide the text into different units of meaning and summarize each unit as briefly as possible.
7. To what extent could the style of the text be considered as a mixture of formal and informal English? What is the effect of this style on the reader?

Text form

8. It is obviously the writer's intention to inform the reader about the development of the mod movement. What techniques does he use to convey his information?

Appreciation and comment

9. For what reasons do you think young people tend to establish group cultures that set them apart from adults?
10. Explain to what extent the development described in the text may have influenced the youth culture in your own country. Do not forget to take status symbols into consideration.

Exercises

1. Write a short summary of the text avoiding direct speech.
2. Write down brief notes about the youth culture in your own country. Then give a five minute talk on the subject.

The Bar Mitzvah Boy

66. Ext. Children's playground.

[ELIOT *is still sitting in the same place, watching the group of kids playing.*
LESLEY *enters the playground.* ELIOT *spot her peering round searching for him and immediately puts on his Mickey Mouse mask.*
LESLEY *sees him, and immediately knows it's him. She strolls unhurriedly over to him and sits beside him.*
A pause. They both sit watching the children.]

LESLEY: I should always wear it. It's a hell of an improvement.

[*He at once takes it off.*
They sit watching the children.]

Having a terrific time, are you? We've had a terrific time. We went to the synagogue. It was a good laugh. Pity you couldn't stay.

[ELIOT *seems to have decided never to speak again. He sits watching the children.*]

Listen, Nutcase. There are two alternatives. Either we talk, or I smash your face in. It's entirely up to you. [*No reply.*] In a minute, there'll be *one* alternative.

ELIOT: Are they upset?

LESLEY: 'Upset'?

ELIOT: Are they?

LESLEY: Oh, brilliant! No, they're having bloody singsong! Eliot – for God's sake – the most important day of their lives!

[*A pause.*]

Well?

[ELIOT *shrugs. Then sighs.*]

ELIOT: I went for a haircut by the way.

LESLEY: You what??

ELIOT: I didn't have one though.

LESLEY: You went for a *bar mitzvah* . . . you didn't have one of those either! What the hell do you mean you went for a haircut! Is that why you left? To go for a sodding haircut?

ELIOT: 'Course not.

LESLEY: Well, why?

[*A pause.*
Why, Eliot?

ELIOT: I don't think I'm old enough to be bar mitzvah'd.

[LESLEY *stares at him, completely nonplussed.*]

LESLEY: You're thirteen. That's the *age*.

ELIOT: I don't think I've got the qualifications.

LESLEY: *What* qualifications? The only qualification is to be thirteen! All you've to do is breathe for thirteen years and avoid the *traffic*! What the hell are you talking about?

(*A pause.*
A ball rolls towards them, accidentally thrown there by a couple of kids playing. ELIOT *picks it up and throws it back to them.*]

ELIOT: I don't think I believe in them, Lesley.

LESLEY: In what?

ELIOT: Bar mitzvahs. I don't think they work.

LESLEY [*confused, exasperated*]: Eliot. Every Jewish boy gets bar mitzvah'd. Every single one. For thousands of years!

ELIOT [*helpfully*]: Five thousand seven hundred and thirty six.

LESLEY [*accepting his help*]: Five thousand seven hundred and thirty six. Everybody. Dad did it. Grandad. Harold . . .

ELIOT: They're not men, Lesley.

[*The simple sentence is like a terrible smack across the face. Calm now, very grave, very concerned,* LESLEY *stares at him.*]

That's the whole point. If that's being a man, I don't want to be one, do I? And it was no good pretending I did.

[*A pause.*
LESLEY *is beginning to understand the truth of what he's said. It hurts her and saddens her.*]

LESLEY [*lamely*]: What are they then? If they're not men? Giraffes?

[*A pause.*
The ball comes rolling towards them again from the two children playing. They're both too preoccupied to return it.]

FIRST KID [*calling*]: Can we have our ball back, missus? [*Pause.*] Oy! Grandma! Cloth-ears!

[LESLEY, *absently, throws it back to them.*]

LESLEY [*apprehensive about what* ELIOT *may reply*]: Dad's a man, Eliot . . .

ELIOT [*calmly, reasonably; he's thought it all out many times before*]: If he was my age and behaved like he does, he'd get a clip round the ear. Dad's a big spoilt kid, Lesley. Do you know why I wouldn't go for a haircut yesterday? Because everybody wanted me to. I was being a stupid kid. Awkward. Like dad. He doesn't care tuppence what other people want. That's ignorant, really, in a grown man.

[*A pause.*]

LESLEY [*even more apprehensively*]: And Harold?

ELIOT: Harold does everything that everybody wants. That's even worse. He's scared *not* to. He's scared all the time. *You* ought to know. [*Pause.*] Grandad wants everybody to think the world of him just because he's Grandad. Just because he's there. Like babies do. Little babies in prams.

[*A pause.*
LESLEY *knows it's all true. The more certain she is, the angrier she feels towards* ELIOT: *she wants to lash out wildly.*]

LESLEY: And that's what you think, is it?

ELIOT [*sadly*]: Rotten, isn't it? It makes my chest hurt.

LESLEY: It's your considered opinion?

ELIOT: I'm not saying they're the only ones. That's the trouble. It's every feller you . . .

LESLEY: Well, here's *my* considered opinion, Eliot. You're a bloody liar! It's all an excuse, you lying sod! You ran away because you couldn't do it! Because you were frightened you'd forgotten what you'd learnt!

ELIOT: I wasn't, Lesley.

LESLEY: You thought you'd get it all wrong! That you'd make a nudnik of yourself! You were chicken!

ELIOT [*wearily*]: Lesley, I could do it standing on my head.

LESLEY: Go on, then! Prove it!

ELIOT: Look, all I'm saying is . . .

LESLEY: I know what you're saying! That all the men you've ever known . . . and your own dad, and Grandad, and Harold . . . all did what you couldn't! What you weren't even man enough to *try*!

ELIOT: They did . . . but they *didn't* . . . [*With growing frustration*] . . . they didn't mean what they . . .

LESLEY: They *tried*! They're *still* bloody trying for all you know! *You* didn't! And they're the babies? You're a liar, Eliot. The whole thing's an excuse. You're a bloody liar.

[*A pause.*]

ELIOT [*almost to himself*]: I could do it standing on my head . . .

[*A pause.*
LESLEY *watches the kids playing, then, as though she considers the discussion over, she gets up and starts brushing grass from her clothes, apparently ready to leave.*
ELIOT *sits staring ahead at the children playing. After a moment or two, he gets to his feet, puts his hands on the ground and levers himself up so that he's standing on his head. He begins to recite the first Hebrew blessing of his bar mitzvah.*
LESLEY *stares at him, blankly.*]

Vocabulary

Ext exterior – *terrific* great, marvellous – *nutcase* (sl.) stupid person – *to shrug (o.'s shoulders)* (= die Schulter zucken) – *sodding* (sl.) silly, stupid – *nonplussed* puzzled – *exasperated* [ig'zaːspəreitid] irritated – *preoccupied* busy thinking – *apprehensive* worried – *a clip round the ear* (infml) quick blow on the ear – *to lash out* to attack violently with words – *feller* (infml) fellow – *sod* (sl.) silly person – *nudnik* (sl.) fool – *to lever o.s. up to* lift o.s. – *blankly* without expression

Text analysis

Comprehension

1. Why has Lesley come to join her brother in the children's playground and how does she open the conversation?
2. For what reasons did Eliot run away from the bar mitzvah ceremony?
3. What attitudes do Lesley and Eliot take towards the grown-up men in their family?
4. What does Eliot want to prove by standing on his head?

Structure and style

5. Try to subdivide the scene into smaller units and give reasons for your decision.
6. Find evidence to prove that the language used is informal spoken (British) English.
7. The setting, the Mickey Mouse mask, and the bar mitzvah ceremony have symbolic value. Explain their significance.

Text form

8. What constitutes this text as a scene from a play?

Appreciation and comment

9. Characterise Lesley and Eliot on the basis of this scene.
10. Explain in more general terms what Eliot criticizes about grown-ups.
11. What qualities should distinguish an adult from an adolescent?

Exercises

1. Lesley writes a letter to his parents about her talk with Eliot. Write the letter.
2. Make a list of rules that you would like adults to follow. Consider various ways of expressing such rules.
3. Invent a short dialogue between Eliot and his father (Harold/Grandad), in which Eliot voices his criticism and the person in question tries to defend himself. Try to use the same style as in the scene.

8

A room of one's own

[From a tape-recorded conversation between five sixteen-year-old girls during an English lesson. A, B, C, D and E stand for the names of the speakers; words in brackets are interruptions.]

A Have you ever . . . you know . . . sort of . . . Mum's said to you, like, Could you help me clear up? So you say, Yes, O.K., and you put your brother's or sister's things away, and then they come up and they say, Where's so and so? (Yeah . . . Yes) But then you think to yourself, Well, it's annoying to have . . . to have . . . to leave somebody's coat or something in the middle of the room . . . (Yes . . . Yes, I know . . .) Do you know what I mean?

B And when they do complain, you feel as if you haven't done your job, but then you say, Well, I did pack it away, didn't I? . . . You know . . . what are they complaining about?

D It's annoying as well. . . .

E I do the same . . . I mean if I find anything lying around . . . if it's no good I just throw it away. . . .

A It might mean a lot. . . .

D I think in my family . . . I think my mother is the most consideratc . . . she'd ask rather than my father . . . my father wouldn't.

A Well, I'm lucky . . . I've got a room of my own . . . so. . . .

D I'd like a room of my own, but then again, you don't keep everything in your room, do you? My dad or mother goes in there and finds anything that she doesn't think is necessary . . . my mother would ask me first, but my dad. . . .

B Well, frankly, my mother wouldn't touch anything in my room, you know . . . she just doesn't. She feels I've put it there for some purpose . . . but again, if I go into her bedroom . . . (Yeah . . . That annoys me. . . .) But say if I have a day off from school . . . or when . . . or we've got some sort of holiday and I see things around and I say, well, you know, I'll give the place a good old clean, at least it'll help . . . and I put things neatly, it's all tidy . . . I wouldn't throw anything out, because I'm not sure whether she wants it or not . . . and then she comes home, she says, Where's this? where's that? . . . I feel awful. . . .

D And you feel that . . . um . . . she doesn't appreciate. . . .

B . . . appreciate, you know . . . I even the other day moved her bedroom . . . er . . . (Furniture) . . . furniture around.

D I did that in my house. . . .

B I did . . . I thought it looked awful where it was, you know.

A But I . . . what annoys me is my room . . . is my room. . . . If . . . if it's in a muddle I know where everything is . . . I like my room to be in a mess.

B But you see, we . . . I keep that as a sort of main bedroom, you know . . . (main room . . .) Yes, sometimes I don't even sleep in my room, it's so cold. . . .
C Ooh, crumbs!
B How do you feel on this subject, Pamela?
D [with a great guffaw] Negative!
C I always know where everything is in my room even if it is untidy, but my mother comes along and I can't find anything anywhere.
A I like it when you get to that age where your parents seem to realize that you're . . . you're going off on your own . . . (Yes . . . You're growing up . . .) . . . you've got your own life to lead, so you think, Right, we'll leave all her things, she can do what she likes with them. It's her time, she can do what she likes with her time.
B They start from a certain point, don't they?
E Well, I don't think they always do that. . . . They try ro remember that you're growing up and then they forget.
D Yes . . . they try to protect you. . . .
E They're treating you like children and telling you where to put things. . . .
C . . . going round tidying up after you.

Vocabulary

considerate [kən'sidərit] thoughtful of the rights or feelings of others – *neat* tidy, proper – *to appreciate* to judge rightly the value of – *in a muddle* untidy – *ooh, crumbs* (exclamation of surprise) – *guffaw* [gʌ'fɔː] loud laughter

Text analysis

Comprehension

1. What do the girls often have to do at home and why do they complain about it?
2. Which of the girls have a bedroom of their own and why do they think this is an advantage?
3. To what extent do the parents respect the girls' privacy?
4. How would the girls like to be treated by their parents and how do they explain their parents' failure in this respect?

Structure and style

5. Try to determine in what way the text is structured.
6. Enumerate all the markers of informal spoken English to be found in the text.
7. Why is the girls' conversation rather difficult to follow?

Text form

8. *Dialogue* may be called the main element in drama. The above text is also dialogue. Point out the differences between the two. (Take "Bar Mitzvah Boy" into consideration)

Appreciation and comment

9. Discuss the problems that may arise if adolescents have no rooms of their own.
10. What rights do parents have to intrude upon their children's privacy?

Exercises

1. Some people claim that slovenliness makes life more pleasant. Discuss.
2. Write down what you consider to be advantages/disadvantages of sharing a room with your brother/sister.

at school

9

A research team interviewed 246 young men aged 14–20 living in Bethnal Green in East London. They were selected as being a reasonably representative cross-section of the young people living in the district. They were asked about the work they had done at school.

We asked the boys about the 'usefulness' of their lessons. Over half, both at school and at work, said the lessons were 'quite useful'. The general tone, however, was less complacent than this may suggest; most of the boys who said 'quite useful' did have complaints – 'Some of the subjects are a waste of time'; 'A lot of it was pointless.'

Despite the similarities in the proportions who were approving or critical of the various types of school, the comments varied markedly. The grammar schoolboys who spoke enthusiastically, for instance, often specifically mentioned the value of the G.C.E., as well as of their education more generally:

'You get a chance to ask questions at school and to find out things that would take an awful lot of time to find out for yourself. I assume I've got some intelligence, and the school can help you to use it – I got seven "O" levels, and I'm now preparing for my "A" levels. I think the school has given me a broader outlook on life as well – more of an appreciation of different things. And because of having a higher education, I can talk to all sorts of people.' (17, *grammar.*)

Present and former boys from comprehensive schools more frequently mentioned the vocational usefulness of their courses.

'I'm getting on all right at school. I want to be a draughtsman, and what we're doing at school is useful – it's all technical.' (15, *comprehensive.*)

Some also mentioned more general benefits. An 18 year old, formerly at a mixed comprehensive school, said:

'For printing, which is what I went into, the technical lessons were very useful. The English helped me too – the way I speak – and, apart from the actual lessons, I learnt concentrating, which is useful.'

The secondary modern boys who felt their education useful to them usually made more modest claims for it. Some, like those from comprehensive schools, did talk about the value of technical courses – 'I want to be a tool-maker and they're teaching me how to make tools' (14 year old); 'The lessons were quite useful to me because in my job I have to do technical drawing and I need quite a lot of maths' (16 year old). More expressive of the general view taken by ex-secondary modern boys was the remark of one, now aged 20, who said, 'The lessons were useful for the type of brain we had – only basic English and basic arithmetic.'

Grammar school critics often mentioned, in particular, subjects they regarded as dead or out of date. 'What use is Latin to me?' said one boy. And another – 'I'll never be a Frenchman as long as I live, what's the use of me learning French?' Yet another – 'I'm not interested in reading Shakespeare or anybody like that; I'm just not interested because they're out of date. I haven't got much time for tradition or the past.'

The comprehensive and secondary modern critics also felt that much of their course was remote from life. But the complaint was not so much that the subjects were part of an out of date or irrelevant culture, though this was sometimes said. It was more often that the school simply provided no practical training. The secondary modern boys, particularly, complained that the lessons were of no use in their job.

'Most boys at my school, their attitude was this isn't going to help me when I leave school so I won't bother. The school didn't give you enough scope on trades – it was nothing to do with your job later on. Maths, history – all that crap; anyway half the time I didn't know what they were talking about, to tell you the truth.' (19, *ex-secondary modern.*)

Another former secondary modern pupil, aged 16, said about history:

'History was horrible; it drove you up the wall. He'd write something on the wall and you just had to take it down in your books. Bloody Napoleon and all that crap. We'd say, "We ain't got no interest in this," and he'd say, "Then you've got to find interest; it may come in useful to you." So I said, "I ain't leaving the country," and he said, "Don't you ever read the papers? Perhaps it will help you to read what's in there." Yes, he said all that junk would help you read the papers.'

A common theme among former and present secondary modern boys was that, in general, the school curriculum was dull or uninteresting.

'It's dreary, it's a drag. I'd like to get out to work and earn some money.' (15, *secondary modern.*)

'It was the same thing every day – dead boring, dead dull. I didn't pay much attention. It's just a laugh, really, because they never learned us nothing. Mostly it was a waste of time. I didn't go to school all that much, to tell you the truth. At one time I stayed away a bit too much, and the teacher said, "You'll have to shoot in a bit more often." (17, *ex-secondary modern.*)

Vocabulary

complacent [kəm'pleisnt] pleased, contented – *G.C.E.* (General Certificate of Education) examination set by universities and taken at schools by pupils at the age of 15 or over – *O-level* (ordinary) lower level in G.C.E. as opposed to *A-level* (advanced) – *comprehensive school* school where pupils of all abilities and from all social classes are taught from the age of eleven – *draughtsman* ['dra:ftsmən] person designing (technical) drawings – *remote* far away, distant – *scope* space or chance for action or thought – *crap* (sl.) nonsense – *junk* old, useless things – *dreary* (infml) dull, boring – *a drag* boring, uninteresting

Text analysis

Comprehension

1. How do the boys interviewed generally feel about their lessons?
2. What do they specifically think about the positive value of their schooling?
3. What criticism of the different types of school do they voice?

Structure and style

4. Describe the composition of the text.
5. Compare the different quotations with regard to style. State in what way they mirror social background.
6. From the text make a list of vocabulary that belongs to the register of education.

Text form

7. Explain what distinguishes this text from an interview.

Appreciation and comment

8. Having read the article, what advantages and disadvantages do you see of the type of school you attend?
9. Discuss to what extent the authorities should take the pupils' criticism into consideration.
10. Does school prepare you for life? Discuss (in class).

Exercises

1. Write down 12 different questions that the interviewers might have asked the boys. Then act out the interview.
2. In what way does your school train you in view of your future profession or trade? Write an essay on the subject.
3. Turn the statements of the grammar school and comprehensive school boys into reported speech with the introductory verbs in the past tense (e.g. he said that . . .)

10

Elvis Presley

Two minutes long it pitches through some bar:
Unreeling from a corner box, the sigh
Of this one, in his gangling finery
And crawling sideburns, wielding a guitar.

The limitations where he found success
Are ground on which he, panting, stretches out
In turn, promiscuously, by every note.
Our idiosyncrasy and our likeness.

We keep ourselves in touch with a mere dime:
Distorting hackneyed words in hackneyed songs
He turns revolt into a style, prolongs
The impulse to a habit of the time.

Whether he poses or is real, no cat
Bothers to say: the pose held is a stance,
Which, generation of the very chance
It wars on, may be posture for combat.

Vocabulary

to pitch to sound at a high pitch – *to unreel* (= abspulen) – *gangling* awkwardly thin – *finery* beautiful clothes too grand for the occasion – *sideburns* (= Koteletten, Backenbart) – *to wield (a weapon/power)* to control the action of – *to pant* to take short, quick breaths – *promiscuous* confused and disorderly, unsorted – *idiosyncrasy* [idiə'siŋkrəsi] peculiarity of a person – *dime a* coin worth 10 cents – *to distort to* twist out of shape – *hackneyed* used too often, trite – *to prolong* [prəu'lɔŋ] to make last longer – *cat* (sl.) man, jazz musician – *stance* way of standing, position – *posture* ['pɔstʃə] attitude, way of holding the body

Text analysis

Comprehension

1. Briefly state in your own words what the poem says about Elvis Presley.
2. Paraphrase each sentence in your own words.

Structure and style

3. Describe the outward form of the poem. Consider subdivision, rhyme, rhythm, imagery.
4. To what extent does the poet make use of depreciative vocabulary? (Use different dictionaries!)
5. Describe the sentence structure in each stanza and discuss its significance.

Text form

6. Poetry is condensed language. Discuss this statement with reference to the above poem.

Appreciation and comment

7. What attitude does the poet adopt towards Elvis Presley?
8. To what extent is the poet suggesting that E. Presley symbolizes the attitude of the younger generation?
9. Why do young people often identify with pop stars?

Exercises

1. Write a detailed interpretation of the poem.
2. Explain why you like the songs/music of your favourite pop star.
3. Group work: Try to translate the poem into your own language. Compare and discuss different versions.

11

For what purpose was I born?

For what purpose was I born? I don't see.
To speak words that no one will listen to
No matter how loud I shout them?
To throw up dates, and events
just as I recorded them and be pronounced
a genius? To sit through school day after
day and be referred to as a "good child"?
To hear things that I shouldn't and then be
instructed to forget?

For what reason am I living? To see
man destroy each other, and we listen
to them preach godlyness and good-will?
To take things as they are and never question?
To live a clean life, only to rot away in your
grave? To have things your soul desires, prohibited?
To be told God is good, but disregard the fact
that the world – his so-called "creation"
is bad?

But these are thoughts I must
not think if I am to survive.

V. B. (age 14)

Vocabulary

to pronounce to call – *to rot away* (= verwesen, verfallen)

Text analysis

Comprehension

1. Explain what the poem is about.

Structure and style

2. Describe the composition of the poem. Study the use of: subdivision, rhyme, rhythm, sentence types, enjambment, anaphora
3. To what extent and what effect are contrast and paradox used in the poem?

Text form

4. To what extent can one justify calling the text a poem?

Appreciation and comment

5. Analyse the feelings presented in the poem and try to explain what experiences may have induced them.
6. Comment on the last two lines of the poem.

Exercises

1. Write a short paragraph about your understanding of "a good child".
2. Practice reading the poem aloud. Then give a competent recital which brings out ist meaning to maximum effect.

III.

Experience and problems

12 Leaving Home

Many young people determine to leave home so that they can seek their fortunes in London.

John Wain in The Contenders describes one such man, Robert Lamb, a designer in Ned Roper's pottery business. These two went to school together with Joe Shaw, a reporter on the local newspaper. In a pub Robert tells Joe that a kiln at the factory has been wrongly fired so that hundreds of pounds' worth of pottery would have to be thrown away.

I thought quickly. Roper's, like any small firm at that time, was already riding pretty low in the water; an extra burden like this could sink it, unless Ned could be clever about getting help from the bank or something.

'This isn't good,' I said.

'Cheer up,' said Robert. He drained his pint sturdily, as if suddenly waking up to the fact that it was beer and deserved to be swigged with an air. 'It'll be a valuable lesson to Ned at the outset of his career. It'll teach him to employ good workmen who know how to fire a kiln.'

'Anybody can spoil a kiln now and again, and you know it,' I said. 'This won't teach Ned anything except how to grow ulcers.'

Robert laughed, and called the landlord over to fill our mugs. His whole bearing had altered suddenly.

'Fortunately I can help him,' he said, turning to me with my mug in his outstretched hand.

I was too startled to think of taking it. 'Help him?'

'Save him some money.'

'Oh.' I took the beer. 'So it *is* an idea of yours that's the news scoop.'

'In a way,' Robert smiled. He raised his glass. 'Wish me luck.'

'Doing what?'

'Going to London.'

I was disappointed. Why, even people like me, who didn't *expect* to have any colour in their lives, went to London. I had been several times. 'How long for?' I asked him.

'For good, you ass. I'm leaving Ned's.'

'Dash my rags,' I said. I looked at him attentively, but he obviously wasn't fooling. Some of the wild look had come back into his eyes, too, as if the seriousness of what he was doing was building up a pressure inside him. Yet he seemed quite steady.

'I give you a toast,' he said. 'My London period.'

'Your London period,' I said, and we drank.

In the silence that followed, we thought of London, the impossible London of the provincial adolescent, the smoky swamp full of jewelled toads, the dirt-track where racing taxis full of millionaires skid together in a shower of sovereigns, the pallid aviary of bank notes flapping their wings in time to the cunning chimes of Big Ben.

Still, we couldn't stay inside this reverie for long, in the face of the pressing realities, and after a minute or two I asked Robert to try and explain his motive in going.

'Don't start telling me it's a case of pure consideration for Ned,' I said. 'It's nice of you to spare him the expense of your wages, but that can't be all.'

For an instant Robert looked as if he were about to flare up, and either tell me to mind my own business or insist that the whole thing *was* pure altruism; but before a word came out he had changed his mind, and he merely turned to the bar, picked up his tankard with a rather weary gesture, and drank from it. He had the air of a man who is turning over a number of things in his mind.

'The point is, isn't it,' I said, helping him, 'that the spoilt kiln gives you a heaven-sent opportunity to get away.'

'That's putting it too crudely,' he objected.

'All right, let's *be* crude. You want to get away from here and go to London and lead the artistic life. But what's waiting for you when you get there is so hellish that even *you* shrink from it. So you have to have some big colourful justification – "I can't be a burden to Ned at a time like this" – to make it seem all right and give you the motive to stifle your hesitations.'

Robert yawned. His tensions seemed to have drained away, leaving him, if anything, rather bored with the discussion.

'Well, analyse it if you like, Joe,' he said flatly. 'I'm going. When I heard about the damage, it seemed to flash on me suddenly how much I wanted to get away. And this seemed the right moment, when I wouldn't seem to be doing it just out of the blue. I don't suppose anybody'll be fooled. I expect they'll all be like you and say I wanted an excuse to go and picked on the first one that came up.'

'What about your people?' I asked . . .

'They'll be asleep,' he said shortly.

For a moment I thought he was speaking in metaphor. It just didn't strike me that he really meant *asleep*. Then it did strike me.

'You don't mean to say,' I asked, 'that you're going to sneak out in the dead of night?'

He nodded. 'What else?'

I understood then, of course. He just wasn't going to put up with all the caterwauling. All the same, it was pretty sudden.

'Dash my rags,' I said again. I took another drink out of my tankard, trying to get abreast of the situation. Then another thought struck me. 'This'll make it pretty hard for you to come back.'

'Come *back*?' Robert asked incredulously, as if I were mad.

So he was *really* going it. Putting a match to his boats and bridges right in front of my eyes. All I could think of to ask was, 'When?'

'Tonight, of course,' he said.

This time I really had to cling to the bar. It was all so rapid. Going off! For ever! Tonight! Impossible to return!

'You're what they call impulsive,' I said, watching him narrowly to see if he would rebut the charge. But he just took no notice . . .

'The strategy's dead simple,' he said, setting his mug down after a long swig. 'The old folks always go to bed about ten. They don't wait up for me. So we'll stay in the pub till closing time, then walk about a bit to give them a chance to get safely off to sleep, then I'll duck in and put a few immediate necessities in a case, and off.'

'Leaving a message written in duck's blood on the mirror,' I said. 'Just what *is* the special satisfaction it gives you to go about the thing in this melodramatic way? You could perfectly well give it a day or two, fix up some accommodation in London, and state your case for going like a normal sane person.'

'State my case!' Robert jeered loudly. 'Can you imagine me stating my case to the sort of people I'm surrounded by? Can you imagine me trying to talk the old folks into it, then talk Ned into it? I'd be so exhausted at the end of that lot that I'd have to talk *myself* into it.'

He splashed a lot of beer down his throat, then banged his mug down. 'State my case!' he cried loudly. It seemed to be the phrase that had annoyed him, more than the suggestion itself. 'That's rich! As if my position was the sort that can be stated . . . as if . . . as if . . .' he went on maundering, dropping his voice to an undertone, then burst out in a loud hiss, 'All I want to do with my case is to *pack* it.'

'Yes, but what train are you going on?' I persisted, still sticking to my role of human ballast.

'Half past eleven,' he answered promptly. Evidently he'd looked up the train; it wasn't *all* a matter of wild impulse.

I held my head and rocked softly to and fro, freshly appalled.

'Look, Robert,' I said. 'For the love of God give it a few minutes' thought. It's a three-hour trip. That means you'll hit London at half past two, having had no sleep, and too late to –'

'Sleep!' he interrupted. 'What else have I had to do for the last nineteen years in this dump but sleep? Even when I was awake, dressed, and moving about, I was asleep inside me. The core of my mind hasn't woken up once yet. It's been asleep ever since I was born, because there's never been anything worth waking it up to take part in. Well, now it's awake at last.'

'All right,' I said pacifically. I didn't want him to work himself up any more.

'Awake at last!' he shouted, banging his fist on the bar.

Vocabulary

kiln oven used to bake pottery – *sturdily* (here:) determined – *to swig* to swallow – *ulcer* (= Magengeschwür) – *news scoop* exciting piece of news – *dash my rags!* phrase used here to express astonishment – *toad* (= Kröte) – *pallid* pale – *aviary* large bird cage – *cunning* very clever – *reverie* ['revəri] day dreams – *to flare up* (here:) to become angry – *tankard* mug – *to shrink from* to be too frightened to approach – *to stifle* to suppress – *to sneak out* to leave secretly – *caterwauling* lamenting wail – *to get abreast of* to understand – *to rebut* to refute, to prove the falsity of a statement – *to maunder* to mutter and grumble – *dump* dirty or boring place – *to work o.s. up* to get excited

Text analysis

Comprehension

1. What has happened to Ned Roper and how is his friend going to help him?
2. What is the narrator's attitude to Robert's plan, i.e. how does he judge it?
3. How does Robert explain his intention to leave? What are the deeper reasons?
4. Under what circumstances is he going to leave and what does the narrator think of Robert's decision?

Structure and style

5. Analyse the mode of presentation and explain the function of the narrator.
6. Examine the techniques of characterisation used in the text.
7. Describe the language and state to what extent it characterizes the relationship between the two men. Find and explain images and word plays used in the text.

Text form

8. Point out the similarities and dissimilarities between this text and a dramatic scene.

Appreciation and comment

9. What does Robert expect of London and what, generally speaking, makes large cities attractive for young people?
10. Outline the relationship between Robert and his parents. Then discuss the importance of family ties for young people.

Exercises

1. Write a summary of the passage avoiding direct speech.
2. Read the novel *The Contenders* and discuss the function of the extract within the framework of the novel.
3. Discuss up to what age children should live with their parents and/or be supported by them.

IN NEW YORK: an unemployed teenager can expect to receive:
nothing if he lives at home and has not worked £13 basic, weekly and up to £22 for rent, if he lives away from home; only one in ten get the rent payment
£55.10, without means test, if he is unemployed after six months

IN LONDON: the jobless teenager is entitled to: £9.80 if he lives at home and has not worked since school
£18.00 if he is living away from home
£12.90 if he is unemployed after six months; plus possible supplementary benefit to cover rent. But these extra payments are means-tested.

13

w many careers give you the chance to change your job every two years?

At 18, the thought of doing the same job for 20 years or more can be pretty daunting.

As well it might.

After all, you'll be a different person when you're 40, so why should you be stuck in a rut in your job?

You'd be forgiven for thinking that a career as an Officer in the Royal Navy could lead you straight into just such a rut.

Forgiven, but mistaken.

In the Royal Navy, your first job after you finish training will last only about two years. Then we'll give you a new one.

Two years or so after that, you'll move on to another job.

And so on, right through your career.

Why do we do it?

First, to keep you intellectually stimulated. With a new job to master every two years, the chances are you won't grow bored or lazy.

And second, to prepare you to cope with situations you've never faced before. (We seem to get more than our fair share of these in the Royal Navy.)

Imagine, for example, that your ship spends a short time in the Far East, and you're suddenly confronted with the task of organising a programme of flood relief.

We believe that a wide variety of job experience will stand you in better stead than a narrow specialisation.

That's why your career in the Royal Navy develops in the way it does.

To start with, we'll train you extremely thoroughly.

Then you'll join your first ship.

You could, for example, start off in a Frigate, whose main role relates to anti-submarine warfare.

Later, you could choose to work in submarines, and learn, among other things, what anti-submarine warfare feels like on the receiving end.

Or you could choose to sub-specialise in anything from diving to flying a helicopter.

And in between tours of duty at sea, you might tackle an administrative job in Whitehall.

You could live overseas for a couple of years, on an assignment with NATO. There, you'd be helping to plan exercises which involve the navies of 14 countries.

If you're a Weapons Electrical Engineer Officer, you could move from advanced radar to the Ferranti FM1600 series computer, which controls the missile systems in a Guided Missile Destroyer.

As a Marine Engineer Officer, you could take a course in nuclear engineering, then be responsible for the reactor plant in a nuclear submarine.

You could even read for a second degree.

But starting a new job every two years doesn't mean that you'll start from scratch every two years.

Each new job will add to what you've already assimilated.

The idea is that by the time you reach your early 30s, you'll have seen and done as much as possible.

Because that's when you could be given command of a ship. Or, if you're an Engineer Officer, be the head of the engineering department.

By then, you'll have learnt how to cope with a thousand and one familiar situations, and to deal with unfamiliar ones without running off for help.

You'll have learnt, too, that in managing men, your respect for them is as important as their respect for you.

Because you'll rely on them for their advice.

But, ultimately, you'll take the decisions, and carry the can if things go wrong, and it's your individual judgement that will count most.

The last person the Royal Navy wants in a position like that is one who has forgotten how to think because his job has become a boring routine.

A degree or 2 'A' levels (or equivalent) are required for a Full Career Commission and at least 5 grade C's or above at 'O' level for a Short Career Commission.

Please send me further information about a commission in the Royal Navy as a: Seamen Officer ☐ Engineer Officer ☐ Aircrew Officer ☐

Name ____________________

Address ____________________

____________________ Date of birth ____________________

My present or expected qualifications are: ____________________

____________________ University/school ____________________

To: Captain W.R. Canning, RN, Officer Entry Section, (22 FF1), Old Admiralty Building, Spring Gardens, London SW1A 2BE.

ROYAL NAVY OFFICER

Vocabulary

daunting discouraging – *rut* [rʌt] to be in a fixed and dull way of life – *to stimulate* ['stimjuleit] to excite – *flood relief* help for flooded area – *frigate* ['frigit] (= Fregatte) – *warfare* (tactics of) war – *to tackle s. th.* to deal with – *assignment* job, task – *missile* ['misail] (= Geschoß, Rakete) – *to start from scratch* (infml) from zero or with nothing – *to carry the can* (infml) to be responsible – *commission* (high) rank in the armed forces

Text analysis

Comprehension

1. What age group does the advert aim at and for what reason?
2. Why does the Royal Navy offer a new job every two years?
3. What may a typical training programme be like?
4. What requirements must be met before you are given command of a ship?

Structure and style

5. Describe the lay-out of the advertisement.
6. What gives the advert its personal touch?
7. Divide the text into sense units and describe the logical structure of each unit. Make a list of expressions that help to structure the text.

Text form

8. What constitutes this text as an advertisement?

Appreciation and comment

9. To what extent does the advertisement rely on persuasion and / or argumentation?
10. Could this advertisement lead you to apply for a commission in the Royal Navy? Give reasons.

Exercises

1. Describe the kind of career you have in mind and the reasons for your choice.
2. Should a country have an army of volunteers or compulsory military service? Discuss.

Two girls talking about love and sex

14

JANICE: Love? Well, I don't know what the word means. To me, I'm not sure that it really means anything. Well, it hasn't so far in my life. Not love for a person of my age or a similar age. Love for my parents, yes, but . . .

TINA: What about that boy you were going out with? You said you were in love with him.

JANICE: Oh yes, that was because he'd brainwashed me into thinking I was in love with him. Whereas all the time I wasn't. But now I've got everything straight about that. I know that kind of thing won't ever happen again. But when love does come along, I shall know.

TINA: Yes, it's usually if the boy keeps saying he loves you, you tend to say it back sometimes, but you don't mean it. And then you get to a pitch where you daren't not say it, but all the time you don't mean it . . . And when they realize, they can't understand. 'You said you loved me.' But you daren't say you didn't, because that just proves you're a liar.

JANICE: I'd never say that now. Really, you know, it's taught me an awful lot. I feel that going out with that boy for so long has made me very mature in my ideas about love now, and relationships. I learnt a lot from the experience . . . What I really learnt was that the word 'love' is used too loosely. I learnt what to expect from a relationship, and now I'm using what I've learnt with the boy I'm going out with now.

TINA: As soon as the word 'love' comes into a relationship, everything starts going haywire.

JANICE: People don't realize that you could just go out with somebody, to go out with them, to enjoy their company. But it's never like that. It's always something more complicated. People make things more complicated than what they are. They enjoy doing it.

TINA: They try to define relationships when there's no need to.

Is sex before marriage wrong?

JANICE: I don't think sex before marriage is wrong. Anybody who has had sex before marriage, I wouldn't say anything against them. It's just their personal belief. I don't think I'd have sex before marriage unless I loved the person.

TINA: Yes, but how can you tell whether they love you or not? You get a lot of these boys who say they love a girl just to get into bed with her , and when she says yes they go running to the hair shops or chemist's, or wherever it is, to get the contraceptives, and then, two weeks after, they don't want to know the girl. I think this is a sign of immaturity.

JANICE: Why? Why is it any different whether you do it before you're married or not? It's the same act whether you're married or not. The only reason I wouldn't have sex before marriage is because I don't want to have a kid. If you don't believe in God, are you married when you sign a piece of paper, or are you married when you know your husband?

One young man's attitude to sex

I mean, you lead your own life from the age of about sixteen, or you should do. Anybody else who tries to rule your life at sixteen: well, you can't do it. I mean, you learn off your mistakes, because if you do what everybody else tells you, you never know if you're going to do it right. Not just sex, but life altogether. But sex comes into everybody's life by the time you're about sixteen. I mean, they're maturing more . . . I mean, you see women going round, about fourteen, and, I mean, well they're mature. Well, they weren't like that before. And the older people think it's wrong. But it's . . . everything is changing. Like I say, life's changing. They can't understand. It's changing a lot faster. Since the war it's changed that fast, they haven't been able to keep up with it. We're going into it, and we've got to accept it straightway, from the very start. And you work your way into it, you play around, and then you find your way into it. It's bloody normal. We're not sex maniacs. . . . You go out for a drink, and you expect to finish up with a tart, you know. Not just for sex, just to finish the night off. Make it a good night. It's only bloody normal. I mean, now, nineteen, twenty, twenty-one, that's the sort of ages we are now. Well, I think we know enough about bloody sex to keep us going. I mean, we're not ignorant on the subject, and we're not too far-fetched on it. You know, we don't get right excited every time we see a bloody woman walking down the street, but if you get a girl . . . it's just like they say. It takes bloody two of'em. And a girl goes on it more than a lad does, she'll make it more obvious to the lad, because they're weakest, they can't hide what they're feeling. They're weaker when it comes to sex. Women can't live without sex. They can't pretend to. I mean, it's more emotional to them. You know, it's more within them. I mean, a bloke, they can do it like that, and they don't think any more of it, but a girl has to. With a lad, he hasn't got to go through what she has, when it's finished, it's finished for him more or less. But for a girl it carries on for another bloody nine months. But with a lad (*he snaps his fingers*), he can't help it. It's just life.

Vocabulary

to brainwash to persuade, to convince – *a pitch* a point – *haywire* crazy – *contraceptive* thing to prevent pregnancy – *maniac* madman – *tart* (sl., derog.) girl (usually of immoral character) – *far-fetched* unnatural, absurd

Text analysis

Comprehension

1. How does Janice feel about love?
2. What is her view of a relationship between a boy and a girl?

3. What difference between Jim's and Janice's attitude can you point out?
4. What changes in one's life from the age of 16 are stressed by the young man?
5. Outline his attitude to sex.
6. Why, in his opinion, are girls in a different position?

Structure and style

7. How do key words structure the conversation between the two girls?
8. Are the young man's statements structured in a similar way? Give reasons.
9. Analyse the young man's way of speaking (lexis and syntax). Compare it with the language used by the two girls.

Text form

10. To what extent do the two texts differ in text form?

Appreciation and comment

11. Try to characterise the three young people on the basis of their statements.
12. How would you personally see the relationship between teenage boys and girls?

Exercises

1. Write a summary of the girls' conversation.
2. Formulate the young man's view in a number of precise statements. Make sure you do not use informal English.

The teeny drunks

15

• ALLEN, 13

Allen lives in a London council flat and occasionally attends the local comprehensive. Sue Read met him, playing truant, at an adventure playground.

I'm not a cider basher any more, I was when I was 11, that was my first drink, cider. I got drunk in the school playground. Now I drink sherry and light and bitter. I can get served in a pub, but it's a bit dodgy, so my mates who are 15 go in and get it and we go over the common and drink it–it's freezing in the winter.

I get £2-a-week pocket money from my mum, and sometimes I nick some money from her handbag, but she never notices. I drink when I'm bored, it's something to do. When I get drunk, if I'm in a disco, I just want to dance and dance, but other times I want to smash people up, but I never pick on little kids. My mum says I have to be home by 11 pm, but my sister who is 15, is allowed to stay out till two in the morning, and I say it's not fair.

My mum doesn't say anything when she sees me drunk, though she did the first time. I rolled home and she shouted to my dad, "Your son's drunk, what are you going to do about it?" and he said, "let's see if he can hold his drink, and if he's sick he can clear up his own mess."

At home I'm allowed to drink a pint, no more. If I say I want more they tell me to go and buy my own. My mum did give me a lecture once, told me not to get drunk too often. If I bring my own drink home, my parents let me drink up to five pints, then they tell me to put the rest in the fridge for tomorrow.

I've only stolen drink once, that was from a boy's club. I carried off six crates, but I was drunk after four of them. The best drink I've ever had was white rum, it blew my head off, but I can't afford it. If I go home drunk I don't go to bed, because the room's spinning round and I don't like it, so I watch TV and sit up.

I've been into drugs, I used to sniff ladies shoe colouring, you get a hell of a buzz off that, but drinking's better, you know what you're doing. I mostly drink at the weekends 'cos I get my pocket money on a Friday, and later on in the week I'm broke and I don't like to ponce off my mates. That's what girls do when they drink, they get blokes to buy it for them.

I've never had a real bad hangover, never had to stay in bed, anyway I couldn't with a mum like mine. But sometimes I don't go to school, I've been off for six days in the last five weeks. My mum knows I go into pubs, I tell her. My dad takes the mick out of me, says he didn't know I could get served, but I do, all the time.

I've only ever been ill once on drink, that was cider, two years ago. I drank two and a half quarts a day for a week, and got sick of it. Now I'll drink anything. I bought some barley wine once, it was terrible, I had to hold my nose to drink it, and some nights, when I'm broke, I buy some wine in a pint glass, and go round my mates who are drinking other drinks, and they share their's. So they tip beer, light ale, vodka, all into one glass. That gets me drunk.

I enjoy the feeling I get from drink, it makes me laugh, and I can walk straight. I've been stopped by the police, when I've been carrying a bottle and they gave me a chat about drinking, and ask me where I got it from. But I've been drunk at school and nobody's ever noticed. I like pubs best, they have a certain kind of atmosphere.

The trouble is all the old blokes stare at you, 'cos you're young.

My 15-year-old sister drinks Pernod. She does get drunk, but not very often and no one ever says anything to her. I don't think I'll drink more as I get older, it would cost me a fortune. I haven't got a girl friend, I could have if I wanted to, but I can't be bothered.

Drink's better than most of the girls I know, and you can't drink with girls, they're too sissy. I like drinking with blokes.

• JANICE, 16

Janice is a heavily made-up 16-year-old who lives with her mother and sisters in a South London council estate. Her father died a year ago. She talked to Sue Read in a Wimpy bar.

I was 12 years old when I had my first drink, my mates brought some cider, and we drank it outside a youth club. First of all I could get served in pubs then I got barred when they sussed out how old I was, so I had to find another pub.

When I was 14 I drank brandy, but it was too expensive, so now I drink gin and coke. I always drink in pubs, I like the ones with music, and after they shut, me and my mates buy some bottles and go round someone's house. I don't have any money, but it doesn't matter, because I know everyone in the pubs I go to. Last night for instance, I went into a bar, and got five drinks bought for me straight away.

I'll drink as much as I can get, 'cos I like it, doesn't everyone? If I'm too drunk to get home I stay at my mate's house, but I normally catch the last bus at midnight. In the morning I get up about lunch time, unless I feel really ill, then I stay in bed all day.

In the afternoons I watch the telly, and go out about six o'clock to the pub. The only thing is I do get the needle easy when I'm drunk. I've had three convictions for drinking, the first was when I was 15, there was a fight outside a pub, and I hit this copper, but he ripped my coat, nice coat it was too.

The second time, I said something to a policeman–I can never remember much–but they nicked me for being drunk and disorderly, and the third time was on my birthday, I went into a Wimpy bar and they called the police. I'm on bail now for putting a dustbin through a shop window, but I'm sure it was my mate who did it, I was just laughing, but I can never remember much when I'm really drunk. I've never been given a lecture by the police about drink, and when I go out my mum just says: 'Look after yourself.' But I know she gets upset, and although she never says anything, I know.

My parents never ask what time I get home, because they're normally in bed asleep. My mum doesn't drink at all, we never even have a drop in the house, now and again she sips some tonic wine, to give herself a pick up. My youngest sister, Brenda, who is 14, drinks port and lemon. She's got a Saturday job in a hairdresser's, and then goes down the Palais and gets drunk, but she's never been picked up by the police. I hope she doesn't, because my mum would blame me, she'd say that Brenda was taking after me, and then I'd get it.

I'd rather drink than take drugs, I mean if you take sleepers you just go to sleep, and pot costs lots of money. Because of the trouble I've been in when I'm drunk, I've been in Holloway Prison for a few days, and went into a remand home for three or four weeks, and I've got a £6 fine to pay at the moment, but I haven't got any money. I can't be bothered to sign on for Social Security, takes up too much time. They say I'll go to prison if I don't pay this fine, but I don't know what'll happen to me.

Vocabulary

to play truant to stay away from school – *cider basher* (sl.) someone who drinks a lot of cider – *dodgy* (infml) risky, dangerous – *to nick* (sl.) to steal – *buzz* (sl.) feeling of being high caused by drugs – *broke* (sl.) out of money – *to ponce* (derog.) to live at somebody else's expense – *hangover* unpleasant after effects of too much drinking – *sissy* (infml) effeminate, girlish – *council estate* housing area supported by the local government – *to suss out* (infml) to find out – *to get the needle easy* (sl.) to be easily provoked or excited – *to nick* (sl.) to arrest – *to be on bail* (= gegen Kaution auf freiem Fuß sein) – *pick-up* (infml) (here:) new strength and cheerfulness – *pot* (sl.) marijuana – *remand home* (= Erziehungsanstalt)

Text analysis

Comprehension

1. What is Allan's attitude towards alcohol?
2. How does he manage to obtain alcoholic drinks?
3. What is his relationship with his family?
4. Describe Janice's appearance and background.
5. How does she spend her day?
6. How often and for what reasons has she appeared in court?
7. What is the relationship with her family?

Structure and style

8. Describe the presentation (lay-out) of the text.
9. To what extent are the two talks similar in structure?
10. Why must the language used by the two youngsters be classified as informal spoken English?

Text form

11. The purpose of the news story is "to enable the addressee to form his own independent opinion of facts and events without being influenced by the reporter's references to his own views."[1]
    Discuss whether or not the above text comes under the heading of news story.

Appreciation and comment

12. For what reasons do you think the two youngsters have taken to drinking?
13. Our modern society is addicted to alcohol. Discuss.
14. What measures should be taken to prevent the spread of alcoholism?

Exercises

1. Write a letter of advice to either Allan's or Janice's parents.
2. Imagine you have to defend Janice in court. Write down your arguments.

---

[1] E. Werlich, *A Text Grammar of English,* Heidelberg 1976, p. 69.

TODAY Sue Taylor writes another chapter in her weekly series – A Child in Need.

With the help of East and West Sussex County Councils, the Evening Argus is trying to find foster parents for youngsters in care who badly need the love of a family.

Each week a boy or girl will tell their story. We hope you will help by offering them a foster home.

16

'Loner' looking for a family

by Sue Taylor

AT 15, Vincent is already a loner . . . He has had to face up to a number of bitter disappointments, starting with the break-up of his family over ten years ago.

Vincent and his younger brother were fostered with the same family but although Vincent seemed to settle with the couple and their own children, his brother did not and was moved.

This change was never really understood by Vincent and eventually he and the foster family parted.

So, it was back to square one. At the children's centre where Vincent went next staff saw that he had difficulties making friends with other youngsters.

He often moaned that he was treated unfairly and bullied by the others. When he went out, he seemed happiest when alone.

School

One step towards success was Vincent's part-time work doing gardening jobs for local people which he enjoyed.

He also seemed to like his school and there was never any problem in getting him to go regularly.

Teachers said the biggest problem was his lack of self-control. He was rather intolerant of others and would lose his temper far too often.

Even so, he was fairly friendly with a large crowd of school-mates although he did not have a special friend.

Things have been less happy at home. Vincent – whose name has been changed to protect him – only sees his mother and father occasionally and finds this hard to accept.

In spite of his fantasies about returning home to his mother, Vincent has accepted, at least superficially, that this is most unlikely.

Sailing

At the moment he is living in a children's home near Burgess Hill and has not yet started at another school.

Vincent himself is now keen to find foster parents.

"I feel a bit worried about it because of what happened last time but I want to give it another try," he says.

The tall, dark-haired teenager also told me that he would like to follow up his interest in sailing, prompted when he went on a special sailing course.

His social worker feels that Vincent needs to feel he has some roots and that he would probably fit in best where he was the only youngster around, or just one of a small family.

Foster parents would have to be prepared to give him a lot of time and understand the problems which have made him rather defensive.

If you feel you might like to foster Vincent, or want more information about fostering in general, please contact Trish Osborne, Special Placement Project, Shelleys, Southway, Burgess Hill. Tel. Burgess Hill 42705.

Vocabulary

Evening Argus popular Brighton newspaper – *loner* s.o. who keeps to himself – *to face up to* to be confronted with – *back to square one* back to the beginning – *to bully* to treat rudely – *to prompt* to cause, to start

Text analysis

Comprehension

1. Give a brief account of what has happened to Vincent so far.
2. Explain what is to be understood by fostering.
3. What is the purpose of the article?

Structure and style

4. Describe the lay-out of the article and its effect on the reader.
5. Outline the order in which the author presents the problems in relation to the purpose of the article.
6. Analyse the style of the text and explain why it is characteristic of a popular newspaper.

Text form

7. To what extent can this article be considered as a news story, to what extent is it different?

Appreciation and comment

8. What, according to this article, is expected of foster parents and what other demands should be met by them in your opinion?
9. What are your views on newspaper campaigns like this?

Exercises

1. Write a letter to the paper saying that you are interested in giving Vincent a home. Explain why you think your home and family would be suitable.
2. Discuss the advantages and disadvantages of fostering as opposed to children's homes.

"Wings" 17

"You weren't at the funeral."

He lowered his head, making no attempt to answer. After a minute, she spoke again, bitterly. "You haven't changed a bit, have you?"

Neither have you, he wanted to say. Either of you. But he kept his peace. With Travis gone he just didn't have any stomach left for arguing. No reason to.

"You always were irresponsible. But I never thought . . ."

Tears were welling in her eyes. "I never thought you'd deliberately miss your own brother's funeral. After all he did for you –" Then, suddenly, she seemed to catch hold of herself, for she straightened, some of the iron he remembered so well coming back. "Well, I suppose that's my fault for expecting anything from you. Always knew you'd turn out no good. Not like Travis –" She broke off.

Long ago, before he learned how things worked, he'd been jealous of his brother. Travis had been everything and had everything he'd ever wanted. But after suffering most of his life in a hell of self-pity, he'd learned to stop beating his head against a wall and take love where he found it. Not where it should be. That's how he could stand in front of them without going to pieces.

It had been a mistake, coming back. Why he had was a puzzle even to him; maybe he was just looking for someone to run to. Whatever, the only sensible thing to do now was leave. "Well, I just came down to see how you were getting along." It wasn't the truth, but how do you explain something like that? "I suppose I should –"

"Better get washed." She'd moved over to the stove, shifting pots around. "Dinner'll be ready in a few minutes."

He just stared, trying to understand. But she was ignoring him, so he just threw his coat on a chair. If he hadn't been such a natural-born fool, he would've made a clean break and forgot. But he always had been dumb like that. It was one of the things that made coming down so hard.

He couldn't eat much.

Nobody did; everywhere you looked, there was that empty chair. After pushing the stew around on her plate for several minutes, his mother cleared off the table and brought on the coffee. It was then that his father decided to talk to him.

"They let you stay at the university with that hair?"

It was hard to keep a straight face. The sight of Curtis Younger struggling with his dislike – it touched his sense of humor in a sardonic sort of way. "Compared to some, it's short, Papa." He noted the flicker behind the other's eyes. It always had annoyed him to be called that. By him, that is.

"Then I can't say much for them. If I was the chancellor, I'd kick all you hippies out of there. A school's no place for such nonsense."

How would you know, he asked silently. You never even made it to high school. Reaching for the coffee, he noticed it was in a different pot. That surprised him;

the copper one had been his mother's prize possession. "What happened to your old pot?"

She was scraping the dishes into the sink. "Took it to a church social last month. Someone swiped it right out from under my nose." The clatter increased. "Turned around one minute, and the next it was gone. I found that old one laying around, though, and cleaned it up. It'll do."

By now, the last of the sun was gone. Sitting there in the yellow circle of the lamp, he could almost feel he was home, if he didn't look to the empty place across from him. But something was wrong. Looking up, he found his father glaring at him.

"I suppose you'll be getting a haircut."

He almost missed that. "What –?"

"No son of mine is going around looking like a freak. Tomorrow, you get yourself into Huntington and have Ira cut that mop for you."

He rose from the table.

They expected him to stay. It finally dawned on him, nearly causing him to drop his coffee cup. They expected him to take Travis' place, wearing his life away trying to just clear enough for the mortgage. "Wait a minute –"

"And don't give me any back talk." The look in his father's eyes cut protests short. "Out of respect for your brother. I won't argue with you. But the least you could have done for him was to come home looking like a human being." He cast a last, disparaging look at his clothes.

"Wait –" He was half out of his chair. "I don't want to –"

But it was too late. He was gone.

Slowly, he lowered himself back down, consternation darkening his face. Well, Benjie, he thought silently, you've really landed yourself in a mess this time. He didn't notice his mother watching him, a guarded look around her mouth.

"You don't want to do what?"

His head jerked up.

There was a funny cast to her face, almost as if she were – afraid? Of what? As gently as possible he told her, "I don't want to leave school and be a farmer all my life. I was trying to tell him that, but he wouldn't listen."

It upset her. She tried to hide it the only way she knew how – by plunging back into her work – but he read the signs too well. "You don't like that, do you?"

For a long while he got no answer. Then, "Your place is here, not at some university halfway across the state."

He smiled ruefully. "No, it's not." She gave him a hard look, but he went on. "Let's not kid ourselves anymore, all right? You've never had the time of day for me, and you know it. The happiest day of your life was when I left for school."

She didn't attempt to deny it. In a way, he was a little sad; even after all the years you never quite stopped hoping. But that was the way it was. "So why are you so upset that I'm not hanging around?"

"Your father needs you." Her voice was small. He would've scoffed, but she went on, not giving him a chance. "He's not a well man. Hasn't been for years."

☛

Her roughened hands were tracing the scars in the tabletop, a distant look in her eyes. "You remember that time he was sick, five years ago?"

He nodded. That had been the summer Travis had dropped out of school. It would always stick in his mind because, to this day, he didn't know what made him do it. All his life, his brother had only wanted one thing – to be a pilot. Leaving in his last year had put an end to that. "He had pneumonia, didn't he?"

Her hands tightened around the back of a chair. "He had a heart attack," she said softly.

The words froze his mind. A heart attack . . .

"Travis said not to tell you." Her eyes were welling up again. "You were too young. But ever since then, your father hasn't been able to handle the farm by himself. If he tries, it could bring on another attack. A fatal one."

He was about to ask why, if it was that serious, they didn't hire someone to take Travis' place, when a thought hit him that made him sick – physically sick. "Travis knew everything?" His hand gripped his cup.

She nodded silently.

"That's why he dropped out of school, isn't it?" He didn't wait for an answer. He let you wreck his life because of some warped sense of loyalty . . . Oh, Jesus. He bent his head over the table.

Silence hung between them. Then, his mother spoke again. "What are you going to do?"

"Do?" He looked up, blinking for a moment. "Hell, I don't know. I need some time to think." Rubbing his eyes, "I'll let you know in the morning, OK?"

Vocabulary

stomach ['stʌmək] (here:) courage – *iron* (here:) courage – *to make a clean break* to leave without incident – *dumb* [dʌm] (AE) lacking insight or intelligence – *stew* dish of vegetables and meat cooked together – *to keep a straight face* not to laugh, to remain serious – *sardonic* mocking, scornful – *chancellor* ['tʃaːnsələ] chief administrative officer in a university – *church social* non-religious social gathering held at a church – *to swipe* (infml) to steal – *freak* abnormal thing or person – *mortgage* ['mɔːgidʒ] (= Hypothek) – *to disparage* to criticise, to suggest that s.th. is of small value – *consternation* [kɔnstə'neiʃən] surprise and fear – *guarded* cautious – *to kid* (infml) to deceive – *to scoff* to speak with contempt – *warped* ['wɔːpt] bent or twisted

Text analysis

Comprehension

1. What is the young man reproached with by his mother and what is his reaction?
2. Why has he come home and how does he feel about it?
3. What do Father and son argue about?

4. Why does he think that he has "landed himself in a mess"?
   What do his parents expect of him and why?
5. Describe the relationship between the parents and the two brothers.

Structure and style

6. Subdivide the text into smaller units of meaning and describe the techniques of presentation.
7. Explain why the language used in the text must be classified as informal American English.
8. Comment on the point of view employed in this passage and its function.

Text form

9. Discuss the text form of the passage. Then compare it with "Leaving Home" and "Last Day".

Appreciation and comment

10. Explain the title of the text in relation to the author's intention.
11. How do you judge the boy's behaviour towards his parents?
12. Why do young people's fashions, hairstyles and pastimes often lead to conflict with the adults?

Exercises

1. Write two short dialogues between the narrator and his parents in which he explains to them a) his reasons for staying at home b) the reasons for leaving them.
2. Write a summary of the text in no more than 150 words.
3. Write a detailed interpretation of the text.

Last day 18

Here, in this extract from Iris Murdoch's novel *The Flight From the Enchanter,* a teenage girl from a wealthy home rebels against her expensive school. Because she is a high-spirited, independent person, her rebellion takes a dramatic form.

It was about three o'clock on a Friday afternoon when Annette decided to leave school. An Italian lesson was in progress. In an affected high-pitched voice the Italian tutor was reading aloud from the twelfth canto of the *Inferno.* She had just reached the passage about the Minotaur. Annette disliked the *Inferno.* It seemed to her a cruel and unpleasant book. She particularly disliked the passage about the Minotaur. Why should the poor Minotaur be suffering in hell? It was not the Minotaur's fault that it had been born a monster. It was God's fault. The Minotaur bounded to and fro in pain and frustration, Dante was saying, like a bull that has received the death blow. *Partite, bestia!* said the mincing voice of the Italian tutor. She was an Englishwoman who had done a course on Italian civilization in Florence when she was young. Virgil was speaking contemptuously to the Minotaur. Annette decided to go. I am learning nothing here, she thought. From now on I shall educate myself. I shall enter the School of Life. She packed her books up neatly and rose. She crossed the room, bowing gravely to the Italian tutor, who had interrupted her reading and was looking at Annette with disapproval. Annette left the room, closing the door quietly behind her. When she found herself outside in the heavily carpeted corridor, she began to laugh. It was all so absurdly simple, she could not imagine why she had not thought of it long ago. She crossed the corridor with a skip and a jump, making a tasteful vase of flowers rock upon its pedestal, and went down the steps to the cloakroom three at a time.

The Ringenhall Ladies' College was an expensive finishing-school in Kensington which taught to young women of the debutante class such arts as were considered necessary for the catching of a husband in one, or at the most two, seasons. The far-sighted mammas of the social group from which Ringenhall recruited its pupils were not by any means as rich as they used to be, and they wanted quick results. Ringenhall was geared to the production of those results with the stringency of a military operation. Annette had been a pupil at Ringenhall for about six months. Her father, who was a diplomat, wanted her to 'come out' in London, and had taken the view that a short period at an establishment of this kind would produce in his 'cosmopolitan ragamuffin', as he called Annette, sufficient of the surface of a young English lady for him to be able to pass her off as such during the social season which he felt to be a necessary part of her upbringing, if not exactly its crown. Andrew Cockeyne, who had not lived in England himself since he was twenty-three, and indeed thoroughly disliked the place, which he found, though he would not have admitted it, both tedious and oppressive, had nevertheless taken care to send his son to his own public school. Annette's education, which was less important, and in the course of which she had learnt four languages and little else, had been picked up *un peu partout;* but it was essential in her father's view that it should reach its climax in no other place than London. Annette's mother, who was Swiss, had spread out her hands and assented to this arrangement, and if she had felt any scepticism about it she had kept it to herself.

Annette was nearly nineteen. Concerning Ringenhall she herself had not experienced a single moment of doubt. She had loathed it from the very first day. For her fellow-pupils she felt a mixture of pity and contempt, and for her teachers, who were called 'tutors', contempt unmixed. For the headmistress, a Miss Walpole, she felt a pure and disinterested hatred. 'Disinterested', because Miss Walpole had never behaved unpleasantly to Annette or indeed paid any attention to her whatsoever. Annette had never hated anyone in this way before and took pride in the emotion, which she felt to be a sign of maturity. Against the Ringenhall curriculum she had fought with unremitting obstinacy, determined not to let a single one of the ideas which it purveyed find even a temporary lodgement in her mind. When it was possible, she read a book or wrote letters in class. When this was not possible, she pursued some lively daydream, or else fell into a self-induced coma of stupidity. To do this she would let her jaw fall open and concentrate her attention upon some object in the near vicinity until her eyes glazed and there was not a thought in her head. After some time, however, she discontinued this practice, not because the tutors began to think that she was not right in the head – this merely amused her – but because she discovered that she was able by this means to make herself fall asleep, and this frightened her very much indeed.

Annette put her coat on and was ready to go. But now when she reached the door that led into the street she paused suddenly. She turned round and looked along the corridor. Everything seemed the same; the expensive flora, the watery reproductions of famous paintings, the much admired curve of the white staircase. Annette stared at it all. It looked to her the same, and yet different. It was as if she had walked through the looking-glass. She realized that she was free . As Annette pondered, almost with awe, upon the ease with which she had done it, she felt that Ringenhall had taught her its most important lesson. She began to walk back, peering through doorways and touching objects with her fingers. She half expected to find new rooms hidden behind familiar doors. She wandered into the library.

She entered quietly and found that as usual the room was empty. She stood there in the silence until it began to look to her like a library in a sacked city. No one owned these books now. No one would come here again; only after a while the wall would crumble down and the rain would come blowing in. It occurred to Annette that she might as well take away one or two books as souvenirs. Volumes were not arranged in any particular order, nor were they stamped or catalogued. She examined several shelves. The books were chaotic, but in mint condition, since reading was not a popular activity at Ringenhall. At length she selected a leather-bound copy of the *Collected Poems* of Browning, and left the room with the book under her arm. She was by now feeling so happy that she would have shouted for joy if it had not been for the delicious spell which she felt herself to be under and which still enjoined silence. She looked about her complacently. Ringenhall was at her mercy.

There were two things which Annette had wanted very much to do ever since she had arrived. One of these was to carve her name on a wooden bust by Grinling Gibbons which stood in the common-room. There was something solemn and florid about this work which made Annette itch for a blade. The wood was soft and inviting. However, she rejected this idea, not because the name of Grinling Gibbons carried, when it came to it, any magic for her but because she had mislaid her pocket-knife. The other thing which she had always wanted to do was to swing on the chandelier in the dining-room. She turned rapidly in the direction of that room and bounded in. Tables and chairs stood by, silent with disapproval. Annette looked up at the chandelier and her heart beat violently. The thing seemed enormously high up and far away. It hung from a stout chain; Annette had noticed this carefully when she had studied it in the past. She had also remarked a strong metal bar, right in the centre of it, on which she had always planned to put her hands. All about and above this bar were suspended tiny drops of crystal, each one glowing with a drop of pure light tinier still, as if a beautiful wave had been arrested in the act of breaking while the sun was shining upon it. Annette had felt sure that if she could swing upon the chandelier the music which was hidden in the crystals would break out into a great peal of bells. But now it seemed to be very hard to get at.

In her imagination Annette had always reached her objective by a flying leap from the High Table; but she could see now that this was not a very practical idea. Grimly she began to pull one of the tables into the centre of the room. On top of the table she placed one of the chairs. Then she began to climb up. By the time she was on the table she was already beginning to feel rather far away from the ground. Annette was afraid of heights. However, she mounted resolutely on to the chair. Here, by standing on tiptoe, she could get her hands over the metal bar. She paused breathlessly. Then with a quick movement she kicked the chair away and hung stiffly in mid-air. The chandelier felt firm, her grip was strong, there was no terrible rending sound as the chain parted company with the ceiling. After all, thought Annette, I don't weigh much.

She kept her feet neatly together and her toes pointed. Then with an oscillation from the hips she began to swing very gently to and fro. The chandelier began to ring, not with a deafening peal but with a very high and sweet tinkling sound; the sort of sound, after all, which you would expect a wave of the sea to make if it had been immobilized and turned into glass: a tiny internal rippling, a mixture of sound and light. Annette was completely enchanted by this noise and by the quiet rhythm of her own movements. She fell into a sort of trance, and as she swung dreamily to and fro she had a vision of remaining there for the rest of the afternoon until the boarders of Ringenhall, streaming in for their dinner, would make their way round on either side of her swinging feet and sit down, paying her no more attention than if she had been a piece of furniture.

At that moment the door opened and Miss Walpole came in. Annette, who was at the end of one of her swings, let go abruptly of the chandelier and, missing the table, fell to the floor with a crash at Miss Walpole's feet. Miss Walpole looked down at her with a slight frown. This lady was never sure which she disliked most, adolescent girls or small children; the latter made more noise, it was true, but they were often in the long run easier to handle.

'Get up, Miss Cockeyne,' she said to Annette in her usual weary tone of voice. She always sighed when she spoke, as if wearied by her interlocutor; and as she never cared particularly about anything, so nothing much ever surprised her. This calm indifference had won her the reputation of being a good headmistress.

Annette got up, rubbing herself. It had been a painful fall. Then she turned and put the table straight, and picked up the chair, which was lying on its side. After that, she retrieved her coat and bag and the copy of Browning and faced Miss Walpole.

'What were you doing, Miss Cockeyne?' asked Miss Walpole, sighing.

'Swinging from the chandelier,' said Annette. She was not afraid of her headmistress, whose claims to moral or intellectual excellence she had seen through some time ago.

'Why?' asked Miss Walpole.

Annette had no ready answer to this, and thought she might as well skip a point or two in the conversation by saying immediately, 'I'm sorry.' Then she said, 'I've decided to leave Ringenhall.'

'May I again ask why?' asked Miss Walpole.

She was an extremely tall woman, which was also perhaps one of the secrets of her success, and although Annette, too, was tall, she had to throw her head back if she wanted to look into Miss Walpole's eyes. Annette took a step or two away and receded until the line which joined her eyes to Miss Walpole's made a nearer approach to the horizontal. She wanted to look dignified. But as she moved away, Miss Walpole imperceptibly approached, gliding forward as if propelled from behind, so that Annette had once more to crane her neck.

'I have learnt all that I can learn here,' said Annette. 'From now on I shall educate myself. I shall go out into the School of Life.'

'As to your having learnt all that you can learn here,' said Miss Walpole, 'that is clearly untrue. Your style of entertaining is distinctly Continental, and as I had occasion to remark the other day, you still go upstairs on all fours like a dog.'

'I mean,' said Annette, 'that I've learnt all the things which I consider important.'

'What makes you imagine,' said Miss Walpole, 'that anything of *importance* can be taught in a school?' She sighed again. 'You realize, I suppose,' she went on, 'that your parents have paid in advance for tuition and meals up to the end of next term, and there can be no question of refunding that money?'

'It doesn't matter,' said Annette.

'You are fortunate to be able to say so,' said Miss Walpole. 'As for the institution which you call the School of Life, I doubt, if I may venture a personal opinion, whether you are yet qualified to benefit from its curriculum. What, by the way, is *that?*' She pointed to the Browning, which Annette was now slipping into her bag.

'That is a book which I wished to give to the library as a parting present,' said Annette. She handed it to Miss Walpole, who took it with suspicion.

'It is a handsome copy,' said Miss Walpole, 'We are grateful to you.'

'I should like a plate to be put in it,' said Annette, 'to say it is the gift of Annette Cockeyne. And now, good-bye, Miss Walpole.'

'Good-bye, Miss Cockeyne,' said Miss Walpole. 'Remember that the secret of all learning is patience and that curiosity is not the same thing as a thirst for knowledge. Also remember that I am always here.'

Annette, who had no intention of imprinting this disagreeable idea on her mind, said 'Thank you,' and backed away rapidly towards the door. In a moment she was hurrying down the corridor and jumping into the street.

Vocabulary

to bounce to jump – *partite bestia* (lat.) go away, beast – *mincing* artificially sharp – *contemptuous* [kən'temptjuəs] showing lack of respect – *pedestal* ['pedistl] base of column or statue – *débutante* ['debjuta:nt] young lady of higher social class about to be introducet to social life – *to be geared to* to be connected with or dependent on – *stringency* strictness, severeness – *ragamuffin* dirty young child – *tedious* boring – *to loathe* to hate – *unremitting* not losing force – *to purvey* to provide – *vicinity* neighbourhood – *awe* fear mixed with respect – *to sack* to plunder – *mint* (here:) fresh, unused – *to enjoin* to command – *complacent* pleased with o.s. – *florid* flowery – *to itch for* to feel a strong desire for – *chandelier* [ʃændi'liə] (= Kandelaber, Kronleuchter) – *peal* loud ring – *to rend, rent, rent* to tear – *oscillation* swinging movement – *border* pupil living at a school – *interlocutor* [intə'lɔkjutə] partner in a conversation – *to retrieve* to get back – *imperceptible* not noticeable – *to refund* to pay money back – *to venture* to dare (to express)

Text analysis

Comprehension

1. Why did the Italian lesson make Annette decide to leave school?
2. What type of school was Ringenhall and why did Annette attend it?
3. What was her attitude towards the school and consequent behaviour?

4. What were her feelings on leaving the Italian lesson?
5. Why did she enter the library and what did she do there?
6. What two things had Annette always wanted to do and why?
7. Describe in some detail what she finally did.
8. What was Miss Walpole's reaction to Annette's strange behaviour and her decision to leave school?

Structure and style

9. Outline the plot and state which parts of the passage do not belong to it. Then explain the function of these parts.
10. Comment on the use of dialogue as distinguished from narration and description.
11. To what extent does the author make use of irony and symbolism?
12. Explain how both behaviour and speech characterize Annette and Miss Walpole. Do you think that Miss Walpole is a match for Annette? What weapons does she use to deal with someone like Annette?
13. What does the point of view contribute to the structure of the passage?

Text form

14. Explain why the text might be considered as a short story by somebody who does not know that it is part of a novel.

Appreciation and comment

15. What features of Ringenhall did Annette particularly dislike? What are your feelings about this kind of school?
16. Comment on Annette's and Miss Walpole's views on the 'School of Life'.
17. What do young people often do to protest against educational institutions? State your opinion of their behaviour.

Exercises

1. Write the conversation that might have taken place between Annette and her father after she left the school.
2. Have a discussion in class about the advantages and disadvantages of boarding schools as opposed to day schools.
3. Write a short interpretation of this passage.
4. Write a report of the incidents as Annette might have entered them in her diary.

IV.
Conflict

19

Little Johnny's confession

This morning
being rather young and foolish
I borrowed a machinegun my father
had left hidden since the war, went out,
and eliminated a number of small enemies.
Since then I have not returned home.

This morning
swarms of police with trackerdogs
wander about the city
with my description printed
on their minds, asking:
'Have you seen him,
He is seven years old,
likes Pluto, Mighty Mouse
and Biffo the Bear,
have you seen him, anywhere?'

This morning
sitting alone in a strange playground,
muttering Youve blundered Youve blundered
over and over to myself
I work out my next move
but cannot move;
the trackerdogs will sniff me out,
they have my lollypops.

Vocabulary

to eliminate [i'limineit] *to get rid of* (infml or humorous:) to kill – *trackerdog* dog trained to hunt and search – *to blunder* to make a stupid or unnecessary mistake

Text analysis

Comprehension

1. Retell the contents of each stanza in your own words.
2. State in one sentence what the poem is about.

Structure and style

3. Describe the outward form of the poem. (Analyse rhyme, rhythm, subdivision, sentence structure).
4. What does the use of tenses contribute towards the development of thought in the poem?
5. Find symbols and analyse their meaning.
6. To what extent does the poem rely on contrast as a structural device?

Text form

7. What text types constitute the poem? How are they related to each other and to the point of view employed?
8. Point out what distinguishes this text from a story.

Appreciation and comment

9. Why does Johnny mutter to himself: "You've blundered, you've blundered?"
10. Imaginary revolt and anxiety are the central themes of the poem. Explain.

Exercises

1. Write a detailed interpretation of the poem.
2. Compare this poem with "For what purpose was I born?"

20 *Dear Daddy – Dear Sally*

Dear Daddy,

You really want to know what our problems are? Why we protest, love in, sit down, drop out, get high, rave or simply misbehave? You ask what we are really protesting about? Yet to ask what youth is protesting about is a silly question. It deserves, and often gets, the reply: 'What is everyone else complacent about?' The pressing question I should have thought, is not what now? For there are as many reasons for protest as there are protesters.

I see you are all looking for universal causes of our frustration or dissatisfaction. But the universal answers turn out to be universally facile and universally unconstructive. The permissive society gets the blame, but no one knows precisely who, where or what it is. The generation gap is invoked, but those who believe in its existence also seem to believe in its inevitability, if not its necessity in the order of things. I think it exists to give the middle-aged something to protest about. Every specialist has got specialized answers. When we march, the politicians march with us. When we smoke pot, the doctors study us. When we drop out, the sociologists cluster round. Their views, I'm sure, are to be respected. But they are speaking about us, not for us.

There *is* a gap that I'm aware of, but it's so big you may scarcely see. It's an ideological gap, which means you and I will use different words for the same thing. We will adopt different priorities for the same problem and make different interpretations of the same situations. Above all, we will come up with different answers to the same questions. I don't see there is a hope in hell of your seeing it our way. I'd rather you didn't try, as a matter of fact, because if there's one thing worse than ignorant censure, it's ignorant admiration. And we've had enough of that heaped on us this year . . .

I suppose of all prejudices, age-prejudice is one of the most crippling, matching disillusion with idealism, experience against enthusiasm. It makes so few distinctions, equates protest with delinquency, drop-outs with failure. It obscures the fact that everywhere the protests are continuing, articulate, organized and educated and that we no longer feel hopelessly determined by history. It ignores the fact that every drop-out (your catch-phrase, I think, not ours) is in fact society's failure. That each one of them is concerned with the quality of life, which the stay-ins are in no position to come to terms with. Active or passive, though, we aren't deliberately trying to make things insufferable for society. We are simply trying to be a constant reminder that society *is* insufferable.

My Dear Sally,

It must be very satisfying to know you're right. It's a luxury I've not indulged in for many years now. There's a confession for you – I probably seem to have spent the last eighteen years pronouncing infallibly on what is right and what is wrong. Well, I wonder how many times you caught the lack of conviction in my voice? Not often probably. Eighteen years of repetition is a long time to cultivate a passable air of authority.

You are right though, about the distorting effects of age-prejudice. I appreciate that at forty-one, I may not be your kind of scene, but I would certainly resent being classified as a middle-aged archetype, as much as you would resent being called a rocker or a teenybopper. However, just to make the position clear, there are one or two prejudices I'd like to get off my chest first. For a start I find your mumbojumbo of sacred texts quite incoherent, and I refuse to be blamed for not bringing you up a Hindu or a Buddhist. We had our gurus, too, in our time, but we had to make do with Marx as our revolutionary instead of Bolivian guerrillas, whose jungle tactics you must surely find pretty irrelevant in Hyde Park? If they are the keystone of your ideological gap, I'd be very disappointed. I had always assumed it was made of more original stuff . . .

What you might not have noticed is that you are beginning to act out the stereotypes they have created. If, as you say, we have become the slaves to affluence, you run the risk of becoming slaves to your image. Television creates all things to its own image, after all, and unless your generation is aware of what makes you different from other generations, you are all in danger of becoming irrelevant, of just stewing in your 'expanding consciousness'. Which would be a pity.

If I tell you how I see it, feel free to reject this explanation along with all the others. No one pretends that parent-child conflicts haven't always existed. The king must die, after all, and the old must lose power, but will also struggle to retain it against the demands of the young. The conflict was cyclic, for by the time a man achieved power he was old himself and the cycle recommenced. The new factor is sociological. Affluence has brought with it the realization that you adolescents are a market. You have been exploited and in the process your 'teenage' image was created. The exploiters suffered the fate of Frankenstein – their creation developed a will of its own. You have begun to disseminate not the ideas embodied in the exploiters' concepts, but your own ideas.

So this is the new factor. The young have gained a class-consciousness, in the Marxian sense. Your demands are not for Coke and candies as the exploiters hoped, but for social change; this social change is not just for you, to be exchanged in time for the key of the door, but for all of us. So the cycle is ending. You have, to continue the analogy, taken over from the discredited proletariat the role of the revolutionary class. As one of your more garrulous spokesmen puts it, I believe, you should not be trying to destroy government and authority, but to make it redundant.

I think perhaps you understand all this instinctively. But do you understand us? We are used to thinking that recovery from adolescence was usually spontaneous. It was a great comfort. Now we see you, the first planned generation, with television in your blood and radioactivity in your bones, and we wonder if any of us will recover.

Vocabulary

to drop out to stop taking part in a social system – *to rave* to talk wildly – *complacent* peaceful, contented – *facile* ['fæsail] too easy, meaningless – *to invoke* to call upon (for help) – *inevitability* [inevitə'biliti] (= Unvermeidlichkeit) – *to cluster* to gather – *censure* ['senʃə] blame – *to equate to* consider or make equal – *infallible* never making mistakes – *passable* ['pa:səbl] acceptable – *air* appearance – *archetype* ['ɑ:kitaip] model, original type – *mumbo-jumbo* (infml) mysterious talk which means nothing – *to disseminate* to spread widely – *garrulous* talkative – *redundant* not needed – *spontaneous* not planned

Text analysis

Comprehension

1. How does Sally begin her letter and why does she blame her father?
2. What is her opinion about the gap between young people and grown-ups?
3. Why does she complain about age prejudice?
4. What is her father's first reaction to her letter?
5. What does he criticize about the young people and their idols?
6. How does he see the role of adolescents in present-day society?

Structure and style

7. Break down each of the two letters into sense units and find a heading for each unit. Then state to what extent the letters are similar in structure.
8. What evidence of formal and informal style do the two letters contain?

Text form

9. What features mark the texts as letters? Why could it be said that they are an essay in disguise?

Appreciation and comment

10. What problems are broached in the two letters? Would you rather take the father's or the daughter's view? Give reasons.
11. What is your personal opinion about the generation gap?
12. "Young people should not be trying to destroy government and authority, but to make it redundant." Discuss.

Exercises

1. Re-write the two letters as a short argumentative essay, in which argument is immediately followed by counter-argument.
2. Write a letter to your father / mother in which you discuss your personal problems concerning life in an adult society.

Equus

21

Alan Strang has gouged out the eyes of six horses and is now under treatment in a psychiatric clinic. One day, while his mother comes to see him, a quarrel develops which is interrupted by Dr Dysart, the psychiatrist.

[Lights up on the square.]

DYSART: I must ask you never to come here again.

DORA: Do you think I want to? Do you think I want to?

DYSART: Mrs Strang, what on earth has got into you? Can't you see the boy is highly distressed?

DORA *[ironic]:* Really?

DYSART: Of course! He's at a most delicate stage of treatment. He's totally exposed. Ashamed. Everything you can imagine!

DORA *[exploding]: And me? What about me? . . . What do you think I am? . . .* I'm a parent, of course – so it doesn't count. That's a dirty word in here, isn't it, 'parent'?

DYSART: You know that's not true.

DORA: Oh, I know. I know, all right! I've heard it all my life. It's *our* fault. Whatever happens, *we* did it. Alan's just a little victim. He's really done nothing at all! *[Savagely.]* What do you have to do in this world to get any sympathy – blind animals?

DYSART: Sit down, Mrs Strang.

DORA *[ignoring him: more and more urgently]:* Look, Doctor: you don't have to live with this. Alan is one patient to you: one out of many. He's my son. I lie awake every night thinking about it. Frank lies there beside me. I can hear him. Neither of us sleeps all night. You come to us and say, who forbids television? who does what behind whose back? – as if we're criminals. Let me tell you something. We're not criminals. We've done nothing wrong. We loved Alan. We gave him the best love we could. All right, we quarrel sometimes – all parents quarrel – we always make it up. My husband is a good man. He's an upright man, religion or no religion. He cares for his home, for the world, and for his boy. Alan had love and care and treats, and as much fun as any boy in the world. I know about loveless homes: I was a teacher. Our home wasn't loveless. I know about privacy too – not invading a child's privacy. All right, Frank may be at fault there – he digs into him too much – but nothing in excess. He's not a bully . . . *[Gravely.]* No, doctor. Whatever's happened has happened *because of Alan.* Alan is himself. Every soul is itself. If you added up everything we ever did to him, from his first day on earth to this, you wouldn't find why he did this terrible thing – because that's *him;* not just all of our things added up. Do you understand what I'm saying? I want you to understand, because I lie awake and awake thinking it out, and I want you to know that I deny it absolutely what he's doing now, staring at me, attacking me for what *he's* done, for what *he* is! *[Pause: calmer.]* You've got your words, and I've got mine. You call it a complex, I suppose. But if you knew God, Doctor, you would know about the Devil. You'd know the Devil isn't made by what mummy says and daddy says. The Devil's *there.* It's an old-fashioned word, but a true thing . . . I'll go. What I did in there was inexcusable. I only know he was my little Alan, and then the Devil came.

[She leaves the square, and resumes her place. DYSART *watches her go, then leaves himself by the opposite entrance, and approaches* ALAN*]*

Vocabulary

distressed greatly worried – *to expose* to disclose, to unmask – *savage* wild, furious – *bully* s.o. who uses his strength to hurt or frighten others

Text analysis

Comprehension

1. What different views do Dr Dysart and Mrs Dora Strang take of the case?

Structure and style

2. Where and why is the text argumentative / expository?
3. Find evidence to show that Dora's language is spoken, informal, non-technical standard, present-day (British) English.

Text form

4. Collect all items that constitute the text as drama.

Appreciation and comment

5. Describe Dora's relationship to her son on the basis of the text.
6. To what extent can parents be held responsible for the misbehaviour and crimes of their children?
7. Compare this passage with the extract from "The Bar Mitzvah Boy".

Exercises

1. Pratice reading the passage to achieve maximum effect.
2. Write a short paragraph in which you explain Dora's remark "That's a dirty word in here, isn't it, 'parent'?"

22

Analysis

1. Describe the situation presented.
2. Compare the characters and the developments of the two sons.
3. What do the parents think of their two sons?
4. Describe the composition of the cartoon?
5. Cartoons often voice criticism. What criticism is expressed by this cartoon?
6. What do the drawings and the text contribute to the criticism?

Exercises

1. Write an appreciation of the cartoon.
2. Explain to what extent you are guided by your parents' expectations and wishes concerning your future.

23 The children who choose suicide . . .

from WILLIAM SCOBIE in Los Angeles

IN A WEALTHY suburb of Orange County, south of Los Angeles, a 15-year-old recently drove the family car into a freeway flyover support, killing himself. Later, parents found a suicide note in his room.

At a high-school graduation ceremony, a 17-year-old stepped on to the podium, announced, 'This is the American way,' and shot himself before horrified parents.

After scrawling a message that 'nobody loves me,' an eight-year-old girl slashed her wrists, swallowed the pills in the family medicine cabinet, then tried to hang herself.

'It's like an epidemic,' says a worker at Los Angeles' Suicide Prevention Centre.

School-age Americans – children, teenagers, and college students – are killing themselves at the rate of 5,000 a year in an upsurge of suicide which is at its most serious in California.

Figures disclosed last week show continuing growth in a self-destructive trend that has mental health experts baffled. Throughout the sprawling Los Angeles basin, 109 youth suicides were reported in 1979, up 15 over the previous year. Sociologists believe the figure may in fact be higher since cases are often disguised as 'accidents' by parents.

Among young Americans nationally, suicide is now the number two cause of death– after accidents. The teenage toll has doubled in the past 10 years. In the 10- to 13-year-old age group over the past five years, the increase was 30 per cent. Deaths of children under 10 are almost always registered as accidental on grounds that the youngsters fail to understand the meaning and finality of death.

Several hundred suicidal children between five and 13 have been treated in recent years at hospitals such as the University of California's Neuro-Psychiatric Institute and Irvine Medical Centre. 'There's such a demand for adolescent beds,' says one doctor, 'they're getting hard to find.'

Why, in this hedonistic golden State, are so many children sunk in despair? Psychiatrists blame rising divorce rates and the 'break-up of the nuclear family.' Says Dr Donald Summers, a specialist in the field: 'Most suicidal youngsters we see are from broken homes. Divorce hurts a child – regardless of age– worse than a parent's death.'

Life in the fast lane in California intensifies the problem. Nationwide last year some 30,000 people took their own lives – about 12 per 100,000. In Los Angeles and San Francisco that rate was 50 per cent higher.

'Everyone here comes from elsewhere,' says Ms Ruth Doughton, of the Suicide Prevention Centre.' Southern California has more uprooted kids, more one-parent families, more crowded schools, more drugs, the biggest teenage alcohol problem.'

Peer group pressure worsens the booze-and-pills syndrome, which compounds depression and self-deprecation.

The plague cuts across social, economic and racial lines. In the past two decades, as blacks have made major social and economic strides, the suicide rate for young blacks has risen sharply, Among the least-educated, rates are lowest.

Alarm over the trend has led to creation of hundreds of suicide 'crisis centres' and telephone hot-lines. The Los Angeles centre, operating round the clock, seven days a week, answers up to 50 calls a day, around 18,000 a year.

In California, mental health authorities are making efforts to counter the problem. Schools programmes alert teachers to warning signals and offer counselling to students.

'Befriending programmes' send volunteer workers into the lives of 'loners' – those from broken homes. Pilot studies with 'repeaters' – for every suicide there are an estimated 50 attempts – have been initiated, testing antidepressant drugs.

Teenage Suicide

Kevin is sixteen. He left school in July 1977, and had a job in a supermarket that lasted two months; since then he has not worked.

'I don't know what's the matter with me. I feel as though everybody else is better off than I am. I don't mean money although that would help. Everybody seems to know who they are and what they want, I don't know if you know what I mean. My old man don't talk to me, except to tell me how useless I am. He tells me I can't do anything, I've got no brains. They both tell me all the time all they've done for me, and I just don't see it. I can't do anything, I'm not very clever, I can't keep a girlfriend, I'm not good-looking . . . so what did they do for me? I used to go about with a gang, and we had girlfriends, but I never know what to say to them. If I get on my own with her, I've got nothing to say. If I go out with them once, they don't want to see me again. I get so lonely. I've got mates, kids I knock around with, but all they want to do is smash things up, nick things, sniff glue. They talk about football, I'm not interested. I wish I was. I'm not interested in anything else either. I'm deaf in my right ear, I don't even like discos. What I do, I like to imagine I'm somebody else all the time. I think I might be a hero. I wish there was a war. I wouldn't mind getting killed. I'd like to be a pilot of a plane. I hate me, and where I live and what I do. I spend most of the morning in bed, I had a job in a big store, but I hated it. I was just piling things up and pushing them round the supermarket. It was boring. I think I spend most of my time being bored. I can't see any point in doing anything. That's why I thought about dying a lot. If I was dead, I might know the reason why I was born. I believe there's life after death. I think you might come back as something else. A bird, or a horse or a tiger . . . Sometimes I think I'd like to achieve something. Eddie Kidd, that's somebody I could admire. I had a motorbike, only it got vandalized . . . Eddie Kidd, his life has some purpose to it. But what am I for?

'My Mum and Dad are all right. He's not my real father. All they do is watch television. He's got a milk round, she works in a factory. They just sit there. We live in a flat, it's half a house really. I hate it. Nobody round there is alive anyway, it wouldn't make much difference if they all died. What I'd do, I'd jump in front of a train if I wanted to do anything . . . I can just see it. "He was ever so quiet. We never knew anything was wrong."'

Vocabulary

freeway (AE) motorway – *flyover* road or railway bridge crossing another road or railway line – *graduation ceremony* (AE) school-leaving ceremony – *to scrawl* to scribble – *upsurge* rise – *to baffle* to puzzle – *toll* ['təul] (here:) death rate – *hedonistic* [hidəu'nistik] pleasure-loving – *uprooted* without roots, having lost o.'s family ties – *peer group* group of similar age or interests exercising strong influence on its members – *to compound* [kəm'paund] to make up – *deprecation* lack of respect – *to initiate* to start

to knock around with (sl.) to go out with – *to nick* (sl.) to steal – *to vandalize* to destroy on purpose

Text analysis

Comprehension

1. What facts reveal that teenage suicide is on the increase and how do the experts react?
2. What explanations are offered for this phenomenon?
3. How do the authorities try to counter the problem?
4. Explain why Kevin would like to die.

Structure and style

5. How do text types and techniques of presentation structure the two texts?
6. Compare language and style of the two texts.

Text form

7. What distinguishes the two texts as far as text form is concerned?

Appreciation and comment

8. Outline to what extent the two texts complement one another.
9. "Youngsters have never had it so good." Discuss this statement often made by adults.

Exercises

1. Briefly describe Kevin's problems in neutral English.
2. Write a summary of the first text reducing it to about a third of its length.
3. Discuss what advice you would give to Kevin.
4. Make a list of informal words and phrases used by Kevin.

THE DESPERADOES

24

When the second of the three dances in the set ended he asked the girl if she would like a cup of coffee. She said she didn't mind and they went through into the snack bar adjoining the floor.

'Where are your friends tonight?' she asked when they were seated, with cups of coffee on the green Formica-topped table between them.

'Here.'

'Do you always run around with the same crowd?'

'Usually. You have your own mates, y'know.'

'Do you always go about looking for trouble?'

'What d'you mean?'

'Oh, come on,' she said. 'You know the way you hustled John Sharpe off tonight.'

'Was that his name?'

'Yes. Do you always do just what you want like that?'

He didn't like the question. He felt a lack of the power of argument necessary to defend his position. And anyway, all that had no part in this, sitting here with her. He remembered again the moment when he had driven his fist into the face of the man in the back street and felt no shame, because that part of him, the part keyed to violence, was separate from the part which sat here enjoying being with her. She was waiting for him to say something.

'We like a bit o' fun,' he said reluctantly.

'Fighting as well?'

'We have a scrap now an' again.' He glanced at her face. 'Well, you can't back down if somebody starts throwin' his weight about, can you?'

'But you never pick fights with anybody? You don't start trouble?'

'Look,' he said, 'you've got to have a bit o' fun. You've got to break out now and again. You'd go barmy if you didn't. You spend all day workin' to fill somebody else's pockets with brass, an' everybody allus on to you: the Old Man callin' you a layabout an' a ted, an' the coppers watching you when you cross the road because your hair's cut a bit different. They're all alike: they want everything their way. An' what sort of a mess have they all made of it, eh? Wars an' bombs 'at'll kill everybody if they let 'em off. An' they say, "Keep quiet, don't cause trouble. Just keep out of the way till we're ready to polish you off."'

His fist clenched itself on the table-top. 'Sometimes you feel you just can't rest till you've smashed summat; till you've shown 'em all you don't give a bugger for any of 'em, an' they can't boss you around.'

She sat very still, listening to him, her eyes on his face.

'Suppose everybody thought like you?' she said. 'What sort of world would it be then?'

'Couldn't be much worse than it is now, could it? Nobody trusts anybody. Everybody's out to get what he wants. Countries as well as people. Well I haven't got it upstairs – what it takes to make myself a nice little pile, like some of 'em do; so people look at me as if I'm dirt an' say, "Look at him, a ted, goin' about making trouble." So I make trouble when I feel like it.'

'But what about the ordinary decent people?'

'You mean the stupid ones, the ones everybody puts on? They're the ones the coppers an' politicians push around. Suckers. They're okay till nobody wants 'em. Like our old feller. He goes an' gets himself all shot up in the war an' now he's got one arm what's practically useless. So he gets a bit of a pension an' does jobs nobody else wants and walks about with it all twisted up inside him, hating everybody, including me, because I've got two good arms an' I can earn more brass than he does. An' he calls me a layabout!'

He drained his cup and pushed it moodily aside. 'What you want to start all that for? Why d'you want to bring all that up?'

She looked down into her own cup. 'I just wanted to know about you.'

They sat in silence for a time, then he said abruptly, 'C'mon, let's go dance some more.'

He stood aside at the door to let her precede him and as he followed her he noticed for the first time a small wart on the back of her neck, just below the hair-line. The lights were down in the hall for a slow waltz and, curiously touched by the blemish he had just noticed, he tightened his hold as they moved away together and brought her closer until her hair was touching his cheek. He wondered where she lived and if she would let him see her home when the dance finished. He wanted this very much. He wanted to see her again afterwards, too, and knew he would ask her for a date before long. She wasn't like the girls he and the gang usually went for: she was a few rungs higher up the ladder than them, and sharper, more intelligent. No other girl had ever had him in a corner explaining himself. He wouldn't have stood it from another girl. They were usually interested only in how good a time you could give them and how far they were prepared to let you go in return. They were easier to deal with: they took you for what you were and you didn't need your wits about you all the time as you did with this one. But they were none of them as attractive as she and not one of them had caused him to feel as he did now, dancing with her in his arms, quiet, at peace, the need for violence drained out of him so that he wished the music would never stop.

Vocabulary

Formica (= Resopal) – *to hustle off* to cause to move fast – *scrap* (infml) quarrel – *barmy* (sl.) crazy – *brass* (sl.) money – *allus* dialect pronunciation of *always* – *layabout* (infml) lazy person – *to polish off* (sl.) to kill – *summat* dialect pronunciation of *somewhat* – *blemish* mark that spoils beauty or perfection

Text analysis

Comprehension

1. Describe the circumstances under which the conversation takes place.
2. What clues as to earlier events does the text contain?
3. State in some detail what the conversation is about.
4. What are the young man's feelings while he is dancing with the girl?

Structure and style

5. Describe the structure of the text with regard to techniques of presentation.
6. Discuss the significance of setting and atmosphere in the text.
7. Analyse the point of view and its effect.
8. Examine the language of the text in relation to its function.

Text form

9. Discuss the text form of the passage.

Appreciation and comment

10. Outline and discuss the young man's attitude towards society.
11. Hooliganism and juvenile delinquency must be considered as a consequence of the inadequacies and inconsistencies of modern society. Discuss.

Exercises

1. Write a paragraph about the young man's view of society, avoiding any informal language.
2. Discuss the importance of music and dancing for young people.
3. Why is the relationship between adults and young people often disturbed? Discuss in small groups, write down the results, then exchange your views.

Quellenverzeichnis

Text 1
From *The Psychology of Adolescence, Behaviour and Development,* by John E. Horrocks (p. 4–6). Reprinted by kind permission of Houghton Mifflin Comp., Boston.

Text 2
From *Rights,* by Nan Berger, printed in M. Swan, Spectrum, CUP 1979.

Text 3
From *Study English Stage Five,* by Yglesias/Hagger. Reprinted by kind permission of Longman Group Ltd., Harlow.

Text 4
From *The Language of Teenage Groups,* by C. Adelman, in *They Don't Speak Our Language,* by S. Rogers (ed.). Reprinted by kind permission of Edward Arnold Ltd., London.

Text 5
From *The Daring Young Man on the Flying Trapeze,* by W. Saroyan. Reprinted by kind permission of Faber & Faber Ltd., London.

Text 6
From *Observer Magazine,* 2. 9. 1979. Reprinted by kind permission of The Observer Ltd., London.

Text 7
From *Three Award-Winning Plays,* by J. Rosenthal. Reprinted by kind permission of Penguin Books Ltd., London.

Text 8
From *Language, The Learner And The School,* by Barnes et al. Reprinted by kind permission of Penguin Books Ltd., London.

Text 9
From *Adolescent Boys in East London,* by P. Willmott. Reprinted by kind permission of Routledge & Kegan Paul Ltd., London.

Text 10
From *The Sense of Movement,* by Thom Gunn. Reprinted by kind permission of Faber & Faber Ltd., London. Abgedruckt in: R. Mansfield (ed.), *The Art of English G5,* Schofield & Sims, Huddersfield, [1]1969, 1977, p. 41.

Text 11
From *The Me Nobody Knows,* by S. M. Joseph. Reprinted by kind permission of the author.

Text 12

From *The Contenders,* by J. Wain. Reprinted by kind permission of Macmillan Ltd., London and Basingstoke.

From *Sunday Times,* 14. 8. 1977. Reprinted by kind permission of The Sunday Times, London.

Text 13

From *The Observer Magazine,* 2. 11. 1975.

Text 14

From *City Close-Up,* by J. Seabrook, printed in M. Swan, *Spectrum,* CUP 1979.

From *City Close-Up,* by J. Seabrook, printed in M. Swan, *Spectrum,* CUP 1979.

Text 15

From *The Sunday Times,* by Sue Read, 29. 9. 1974. Reprinted by kind permission of the Sunday Times, London.

Text 16

From *The Evening Argus,* Brighton, 9. 4. 1980, by Sue Taylor. Reprinted by kind permission of The Evening Argus, Brighton.

Text 17

By M. Kitay, from *Sun and Shadow,* Scholastic Magazines, 1972.

Text 18

From *The Flight from the Enchanter,* by Iris Murdoch. Reprinted by kind permission of Chatto and Windus Ltd., London.

Text 19

From *Themes: Rebels,* by Brian Patten (p. 14). Reprinted by kind permission of George Allen & Unwin, Hemel Hempstead.

Text 20

From *Nova,* in A. Levine (ed.), Penguin English Reader, 1971.

Text 21

From *Equus,* by P. Shaffer. Reprinted by kind permission of André Deutsch Ltd., London.

Text 22

From *The Observer,* 25. 2. 1979.

Text 23

From *The Observer,* 9. 3. 1980, by W. Scobie. Reprinted by kind permission of the Observer, London.

By J. Seabrook, from Dickens/Sutcliff, *Is Anyone There?* Penguin/Peacock, 1978.

Text 24

From *The Desperados,* by Stan Barstow. Reprinted by kind permission of John Farquharson Ltd., London.

Der Verlag dankt den genannten Personen, Institutionen und Unternehmen für ihre freundliche Genehmigung zum Abdruck von Copyright-Material, soweit sie erreicht werden konnten. Trotz intensiver Bemühungen konnte mit den Copyright-Inhabern der Texte 2, 13, 14, 14a, 17, 20, 22 und 23a kein Kontakt hergestellt werden. Für entsprechende Hinweise wäre der Verlag dankbar.